PRAISE AS A PARENT, FOR THIS BOOK, AND AS A COACH

Praise from Coach Edwin's daughters:

This book is only a thumbnail view of the sensitivity my dad has as a parent, grandparent and a coach. I am so happy to have my dad in my life and in my daughter's. We have always had a very special bond. The most important lesson my dad instilled in me was to be proud of myself. I took that lesson very seriously, and to this day I always put my best foot forward. In fact, I would recite to myself, "Be proud that you are a Trellue." It became my mantra. There are not too many dads who teach their daughter social skills as well as how to cook, play tennis, sail, drive, change a flat tire, and be responsible. He gave me the tools and love to be myself and to believe in myself. What a powerful gift I was given!
—Helen K. Zimmelman

The lifelong lessons my father instilled gave me structure, and they live in me and in my children today. Daddy contributed his experience through sports, life, and love of family, which motivated me to continually pursue excellence. These gifts, which he gave with love, good humor, and a large dose of Southern values, shaped and have comforted me throughout my life. It is with great pride as a daughter, and now a mother, that I have been able to pass these gifts along to my children, Alexandra and Trey.
—Elizabeth Trellue

Praise for Coach Edwin's book and teaching skills:

I am pleased to have known Coach Edwin for half a decade, initially as an instructor here at The Tennis Key, and now as a wonderful friend. We were actually full at teaching positions and really didn't have any openings to offer him. But rather than just walk away, Coach Edwin's persistence and persuasiveness proved me wrong. Not only have we created a position for him, but also his knowledge and experience with young children have allowed us to excel with a Ten and Under Program that has far exceeded my expectations. Coach Edwin understands a child's psyche, and his ability to communicate with children is remarkable. He never talks down to them and he teaches them to take ownership of their actions. The last words that leave a child's mouth from one of his classes are, "We love tennis!" This can be heard across the courts as parents pick up their children. They see him not only as their teacher but also as a grandfather figure. This connection is special, and learning to connect with each child is what teaching is all about. I hope this book will enable readers to understand and make this connection. I am glad that Coach Edwin has decided to write this book and share his experience and knowledge with us.

—Hai Nguyen, director and owner of The Tennis Key

It would be tough to find a more tremendous human being than Coach Edwin Trellue. Since he moved to California, I have had the pleasure of watching him consistently pick the path of most right. Honesty – check; morality – check; integrity – check; character – check; wisdom – check; and I could go on. Just a flat-out stand-up guy, and I am not surprised that he wrote such an insightful book.

—Steve Bellamy, founder of the Tennis Channel, LiveBall, Shotgun 21, and the Palisades Tennis Center

Coach Edwin has written an excellent book on parenting, especially the value of parents playing with their child and a child's free play. His book gives the reader a good model to follow, and suggests skill sets to develop for your child's self-confidence and to improve on his/her natural talents. His point of the importance of parents having reasonable and age-appropriate expectations of their child is crucial. I have watched him demonstrate his abilities in and understanding of child development that he has written about with his stepchildren and the many children he worked with in Florida.

—Geralynn Trellue, friend and former wife

I think Coach Edwin's book reinforces the parenting skills and beliefs that my wife and I already have, which makes us feel good! Children of all ages need to hear a topic through a different voice sometimes for the "light bulb" to go on! That verifies the value of a coach like Coach Edwin teaching life lessons. I also champion his insight in the value of children playing chess for the cognitive benefit and how it relates to strategy in sports, but also in many other aspects of life.
—Erick Gulliory

Coach Edwin is one of the very few coaches who understands and utilizes all the important elements of fitness training for children. He is extremely passionate and patient, like I have never seen anybody else be. He truly enjoys every new encounter with his little students—every day, week after week, year after year. He enthusiastically passes on his experience and teachings to the children, improving not just their tennis game and fitness, but their entire value system and love for sports and life.
—Suzanna McGee, sports performance trainer certified by the Academy of Sports Medicine

Great information, especially how athletics help children in their overall development. I liked that Coach Edwin included his mother's point of view on the use of toys for a child's development; playing with one toy or group at a time and putting them up before playing with other toys. I liked the fact that he feels it is solely the parents' responsibility to guide their child's nutrition. He makes a great point of parents talking to children not only about nutrition, but drugs of all types at an early age. I found his book to be very informative, and it reinforces what we are teaching our twins.
—Yujana Guillory

Praise from parents of children Coach Edwin has taught:

Simply put, Coach Edwin is the Tennis Whisperer for children. Because of Edwin's coaching, our son Carson has grown in the areas of fine and large motor skills, communication, strategy, sportsmanship, confidence, respect, competitive will, group social gamesmanship, and leadership.
—Kendall Severson

If I could bottle Edwin and serve a dose of him to every child once a day, I would. He inspires everyone who meets him to be a better person and to enjoy life. He may teach tennis, but he also teaches about life, through his game and his example. He values children and celebrates the people they are more than I have seen in a long time. He is one of the greatest gifts my child receives on a weekly basis, and I am forever grateful for him in our lives. He is a true coach and I am proud my son has him as a role model!
—Kris James

Coach Edwin reinforces positive behavior as well as what right looks like. The kids have a good time on the court and he truly teaches life lessons. He asks them if they have had breakfast, brushed their teeth. He takes the wellness approach to coaching; knowing that if they aren't well nourished, they can't concentrate and may not have the energy it takes to perform. For my daughter, Kennedy, this is the first sport that she truly loves for the sport itself. I know that is due to Coach Edwin and his style of teaching her to love and appreciate the details and finesse of the sport.
—L. Mason Schultz

Edwin has a style of teaching that is very positive. He relates equally to kids of all abilities and personalities, and adjusts his approach for each child. This positive approach helped my children develop a love for

tennis. One of my sons is an extremely fierce competitor. He is young and has difficulty controlling his frustrations and emotions when things don't go his way. Coach Edwin worked with him to help my son acknowledge his feelings of frustration and how to turn those feelings into positive motivation to try harder the next time, instead of getting caught up in the negative feelings he would have about losing a point. These lessons have benefited my son in the classroom and in his home life as well.
—Suzanne Mancherian

Coach Edwin's classes are fun and that's what keeps the kids engaged. He has instilled an excitement for tennis in our daughter that other instructors were not able to do. Coach Edwin is able to do this because he understands young kids won't stay interested unless you make it fun.
—Annie Wong

Our daughter has taken other classes before, like music, basketball, and gymnastics, but always got bored and didn't want to continue. But she is very eager and enthusiastic about attending Coach Edwin's classes, even after almost three years. We believe that Coach Edwin's teaching style has a lot to do with it.
—Fred Seysan

Tennis is a sport where success requires a combination of solid technique, athleticism, speed, fitness, and an aptitude for ball trajectories and court geometry. These are things that are developed over time through countless hours of practice and hard work. But kids that go into tennis without the right attitude about winning/losing and the definition of success (improving, playing your best, and having fun) will often burn out well before they are able to achieve their true potential. Coach Edwin's dual-goal approach is great for establishing early tennis fundamentals while cultivating a child's sense of independence, good sportsmanship, and ownership of outcomes.
—Mike Kim, parent and assistant coach

PARENTING:
A Parent's, Grandparent's and Coach's View

Parenting to Maximize a Child's Potentials

By
COACH EDWIN

First Edition Copyright © 2013 by Edwin D. Trellue III

All photos and Print Shop images copyright by Marie Teagardin

Some images copyright by ClipArt.com

ISBN: 978-0-9892052-0-7 BOOK Registered

Proof editing by Cory Jane Birkett

Production editing by CreateSpace

Nutrition input and research by Suzanna McGee

Text design by CreateSpace

Published by CreateSpace

Reference/Parenting/Child Development/Family Development

Printed in the United States of America

ISBN: 0989205207
ISBN 13: 9780989205207
Library of Congress Control Number: 2013941306
CreateSpace Independent Publishing Platform
North Charleston, South Carolina

To Gay and my daughters for their support,
and in memory of my parents.

This book is dedicated to all children, in the hope that their parents will take advantage of what is offered in it and utilize other resources to assist them in raising healthy, happy, cognitive, and physically fully developed children. If one parent is helped in his/her parenting journey because of this book, my goal will be met.

CONTENTS

FOREWORD

Parenting: A Parent's, Grandparent's, and Coach's View offers practical advice to help parents/grandparents succeed—in helping their child develop emotionally, physically, and intellectually in relationships in life. It is a how-to book for those parents/grandparents committed to assisting their children to realize their full potential, or a reference guide for parents/grandparents who realize that raising children properly is "a work in progress."

Coach Edwin has learned the lessons offered through lifelong involvement in the world of sports, academics, and recreation.

Coach Edwin realized that parenting in our changing world could be hectic, like being on a treadmill that just won't stop. Parenting can increase stress levels. There's a growing need for parents to be well rounded in making parental choices in order to avoid becoming burned-out, confused, and having little time for friends and other pursuits in life. Coach Edwin realizes that many parents may also carry a tremendous burden of guilt raising their children that adds even more stress. That's no way to live!

If you read and gradually implement the advice Coach Edwin is about to share, which he spells out chapter by chapter in his book, you'll not only enhance your decision making skills on parenting, you'll far exceed the results you are currently experiencing. Specifically, Coach Edwin will focus on how you can maximize your strengths in parenting, and at the same time enjoy a healthier, happier, and well-balanced lifestyle while raising your child. He also addresses selecting recreational activities for your child and who will guide your child through these recreational/sports activities.

The book will work for you because the ideas in it have worked for parents and children that Coach Edwin has interacted with and coached over the years. His wisdom has been earned by making a few mistakes, as well as by focusing on doing the things that work.

Coach Edwin wants you to know that there is no magic panacea in parenting in our ever-changing world.

It takes real effort and commitment to create a positive environment for raising and parenting children. It takes time to implement what you learn about positive parenting. It can be difficult to rid oneself of old habits, beliefs, and rituals. It is a goal of this book to make the information so compelling, it will galvanize the reader to make and take positive action. It is further hoped that the book marks the beginning of a new mission—one with dedication and good parenting at the core. This is an outreached opportunity designed to solidify good parenting and inspire one to positive action.

Thank you, Coach Edwin.

Brian C. Payne, MD

ACKNOWLEDGMENTS

To my fiancée, Gay, who gave me the courage to come out of retirement after two back surgeries, and two hip replacements to teach tennis again, and write this book. Her support helped me overcome my doubts in my abilities and return to my love of teaching and mentoring children.

To Steve Bultman and Dave H. for their years of friendship and support.

To Suzanna McGee, a friend and the author of Tennis Fitness for the Love of It, who encouraged me to write this book. She holds a certificate in plant-based nutrition from Cornell University, and is responsible for the latest information on nutrition in the book. She is certified by the National Academy of Sports Medicine and is a specialist with over twenty years of experience in sports performance and injury prevention. She is a former Ms. Natural Olympia body-building champion. Find more about Suzanna at TennisFitnessLove.com

INTRODUCTION

In writing this book, I share my experiences as a child, athlete, parent, grandparent, stepparent, and dual-goal coach. Yes, that's certainly a mouthful of titles, but they all have led me to this place of accumulated wisdom and gratitude. I hope that my experiences, seen from multiple vantage points, will help parents to enjoy the irreplaceable gift of early childhood development with their child. I further hope that my book can help bridge the gap for parents in situations that I address and discuss. There is a saying: "You only get one chance to make a first impression." The same can be said of parenting. We only get one chance to parent properly during the most influential developmental period—the first eight years of a child's life. And parents, there are few if any "do-overs."

My feelings and experiences as a young child have deeply shaped the person that I have become. I've benefited from some great counseling that has freed me from a lot of carryover childhood pain. My parents wanted the best for me, yet created some stumbling blocks in my childhood that I was challenged to later unlearn for the benefit of my own parenting and self. Through continual reflection and evaluation of our own experiences we can become better parents.

My dad was a brilliant man and a consummate perfectionist in everything he did. He saddled me with extremely high expectations for perfection in all I did, with the exception of sports. My mother spent most of her time protecting me from the wrath of my dad. Sports became my refuge, an activity into which I could channel my energy. It was a safe experience where I was free to be myself. Only through sports did I learn that it was OK to make mistakes and have fun. I learned to respect the process of being judged on my efforts rather than on someone's expectations of me.

My positive experiences and failures as a parent to my three daughters, plus being a stepfather in additional marriages, provided me enlightened experience and insight about the journey of parenthood. Coaching more than six thousand kids has also given me irreplaceable insight into and understanding of children that have helped me create a successful dual-goal coaching and parenting style.

I have found that an exceptional parenting style enables exceptional results in children reaching far beyond their genetic potential. The opposite is quite obvious. A lesser parenting style will produce lesser results. Creating the proper flexible parenting plan is also responsible for a more complete and accelerated development of a child's brain, physical complex coordination, fitness, and emotional attachment.

Successful parenting starts with a plan before the birth of your child and continues throughout your entire life. Good parenting will help you create a deep attachment with your child that will last forever. Experiences lay the groundwork for memories, which may connect or disconnect you from your child. My experience has shown that a disconnection can start as early as three years of age if there is a lack of attachment between parent and child. Either parent putting work before family time or using an uninvolved parenting style will have the same effect on your child.

I outline a variety of deliberate structured activities that you can use to teach your child important life lessons, to assist in coping and developing problem-solving abilities. My hope is to help parents bring out their child's potential through the orchestration of specific activities and games. I am not advocating that parents be their child's athletic coach. I believe parents should be their child's coaches and advocates in all areas of development and life!

Parenting is an ever-changing evolution, which combines our current knowledge and practices with new skills we must acquire. As parents, it's important to be aware of our child's changing developmental needs. Aside from creating a safe and secure environment for a child, it's crucial that parents recognize their own strengths and limitations as a parent. After you recognize your weaknesses, work diligently to overcome them for the benefit of your family and yourself. Remember, a chain is no stronger than its weakest link. We all have a weak parenting link or two. I certainly did.

My goal in writing this book will be met if my thoughts and observations help even one set of parents and their child along the challenging but rewarding journey of parenthood.

Disclaimer I offer my experiences and thoughts as tools that you may want to consider using as a parent. I am not trying to convey the message that not using these tools will result in your failure as a parent. Your personality, parenting acumen, and insight, as well as unlearning your own negative experiences, will help lead you in the right direction.

Gratefully,

Coach Edwin - (coachedwint@aol.com)

Teaching Credentials

- Played high school and college tennis and also swam in college.

- Coached the swim and dive team at Jesuit High School that won three state and city championships in the 1960s.

- Placed in the top five in the nation in the US Marine Corps National High School Physical Fitness Championships in the late 1960s.

- Coached many AAU (now US Swimming) age group record holders 1965–1970.

- United States Professional Tennis Association 2014 rating: Elite Professional.

- Head tennis coach at Sea Pines Academy of Hilton Head Island, South Carolina, and Beaufort Academy in Beaufort, South Carolina.

- Coached the South Carolina Junior Davis Cup and Junior Wightman Cup tennis teams.

- Coached the Georgia Junior Davis Cup tennis team in 1975.

- Director of tennis camps at:

  Fripp Island Racquet Club, Fripp Island, South Carolina; Palmetto Dunes Racquet Club, Hilton Head Island, South Carolina; Peachtree World of Tennis, Atlanta, Georgia; Kehoe-France School Summer Camp, New Orleans, Louisiana; Palisades Tennis Center, Pacific Palisades, California.

CHAPTER ONE
Athletics, a Parenting and Development Tool for Your Child

Many parents are unaware of the ways their child's development will benefit from early involvement in athletics. Not the competitive aspect as much as the activities of athletics and the platform to teach life lessons. Such involvement can play an important role in addressing a parent's universal concern about the importance of a child getting a well-rounded education, one that promotes cognitive, physical, emotional, and social development. The benefits or deficiencies of his education will be with your child all his life.

I use the word athletics to refer not only to the physical activities of athletes who are proficient in sports, but also those who want to be physically fit, active, and healthy or play sports. I hope to show parents how athletic sports can be used as a developmental tool for their child. With a better understanding of fitness in their own lives, this knowledge will benefit parents who are trying to teach their child about nutrition and exercise.

Sports are a great example of an activity in life that hones one's ability to recognize what it takes to achieve a goal and win. Thus, focus, effort, dedication, and sacrifice are needed to improve. Winning defined by dual-goal teachers is when someone of any age uses focus and effort to learn any subject, and improves in that area of study. That improvement—no matter how slight—should be considered a win. In athletics, a dual-goal sports teacher is qualified to coach a sport and teach life lessons to his/her players. Improvement is the key, along with reinforcing a proper work ethic.

My study of the Positive Coaches Alliance has helped me clarify what I and many other coaches and teachers have done for decades. That is to teach various subjects whether it is music, art, academics, sports, professions, etc., and teach important life lessons at the same time. It may seem to be *old school*, but to us it is a natural progression in developing a child. A child is shaped by the scope of their environment. Let us equip them with the big picture of the world they live in, not just a mere peep of it.

The great lesson for all sports participants is in how to overcome failure. Failure in various areas happens to all of us throughout our lives. In the lesson of coping with failure, the value of an unwavering work ethic is illuminated. Experiencing failure in sports helps prepare children and adults for coping with failure in life, and ultimately helps reduce the frequency of failure.

The benefits of athletics for your child will be almost solely dependent on your parental influence and the type of person you choose to teach your child. Why do I use the term teacher rather than coach? In my understanding, the major distinction between a teacher and a coach is, by definition, that a coach directs sports instruction and a teacher provides education in a much broader scope. Teaching sports means integrating life lessons into sports training, offering broader development than that of a single-goal coach. I feel that this is true not only in sports, but in the pursuit of music, art, and academic endeavors as well.

Is it possible to have a coach who is a good teacher? Yes! They are called dual-goal teachers, and the term refers to someone who teaches a sport or another skill and has the ability to also integrate life lessons into the teachings. With children four to ten years old, the most common lesson I teach is that of responsibility. I help children understand the importance of taking responsibility for knowing what is being taught and not depending on someone else to remind or show them. This self-correction can quickly become a continual pattern of learning.

Any list of college coaches who have been great influences and life teachers would start with John Wooden, UCLA's legendary former head basketball coach. Another on the list would be Mike Krzyzewski, Duke University's men's basketball head coach, and current USA Olympic head basketball coach. In fact, ESPN and ESPNU honored Coach Mike by featuring him in a special broadcast aired June 30, 2011. The special featured his impact in molding character and developing basic values in his students/athletes.

There are some examples of dual-goal teachers in grammar schools and high schools worldwide. But sadly, there are not enough dual-goal teachers making a difference in the lives of children. Throughout the world, there are many educated and passionate sports coaches, but, without a dual-goal teaching model, they are not having the optimal impact on their students. Why wait to develop your little treasure and miss the most important formative first six years of his/her development? I say that because a majority of parents don't start their children in sports until they are between six and eight years of age.

Parents alone can rarely do all the developmental work needed in raising a child. I also include grandparents and nannies as developmental teachers for children. It takes a variety of qualified teachers, coaches, and role models to advance your child's development in many areas. The reverse is sadly true. A poor teacher, role model, or sports coach in your child's life can have an adverse effect. In chapters 9 and 10, I will help you identify a good dual-goal coach and program for your child.

The proper athletic dual-goal teachers can provide a young child with invaluable guidance in many different areas of development. A dual-goal teacher can introduce and reinforce the values that parents have planted in their children. The obvious advantage of having your child in athletics is physical development. But athletics are also invaluable in developing character, including emotional, attitudinal, and behavioral response patterns in children.

Dual-goal athletics training can enhance a child's brain function and ability to learn academically. A child will be introduced to concepts such as playing by the rules and sportsmanship, new vocabulary, and memory expansion. A child in sports learns the dynamics of communication within a group. One-on-one communication is much different from group communication because of the respect and patience needed in a group setting. There is a distinct difference between group communication in a classroom and group communication in a sports setting. In a classroom, children are conditioned not to speak out of turn. In a sports setting, they tend to be less disciplined and to talk without restraint. The reasons are the continual environmental distractions and the lack of self-control.

An important aspect of dual-goal teaching is that it increases the amount of time and exposure that a child has to positive developmental learning. There are a growing number of negative alternatives to participating in sports. These include watching TV, playing electronic games, and any activity in which a child's needs or mood changes are not recognized.

On October 18, 2011, at the American Academy of Pediatrics (AAP) National Conference and Exhibition in Boston, President Ari Brown, MD, reported the results of research findings concerning television watched by infants and toddlers. The AAP recommended that: "children under two years old might experience learning delays if exposed to television. Videos and programs labeled 'educational' just did not have the benefits advertised. In fact, the suggestion of the findings was children under two should be screen free. After the age of two, TV should be strictly monitored and perhaps used only for a brief mommy break. And further, televisions should not be put in the children's bedrooms."

Children participating in sports will also be immersed in learning core values and social skills that are exhibited daily on courts and ball fields, in gyms and swimming pools, and in any area that hosts sports for children four years of age and older. Sports participants quickly learn how to express themselves. Again, learning a diverse array of subjects can only happen if taught by a dual-goal teacher rather than a single-goal coach, where only the sport is being learned.

Of course, let me clarify that an early start in athletics does not guarantee or even hint at a life in professional sports, with its apparent financial and glamorous lifestyle. Often, the unglamorous aspects of fame and fortune are the potential burdens associated with them, including depression, drug and alcohol abuse, and the results of poor financial decisions. In many cases, these problems go hand in hand with fame and fortune.

Athletic ability, for the most part, is dependent on the makeup of a child's genetic potential and learning style. Inborn personality and temperament may have a strong impact on athletic achievement. However, the environment created for children by parents and other role models is paramount for athletic and all other developmental categories. Parents and caregivers act as extremely important role models for the development of a young child's personality. A child from birth to four years of age who is exposed to appropriate developmental activities will experience increased cognitive development compared to a child without that exposure.

Influential activities start with a newborn's feeling secure and nurtured, and being held often. Before your child can walk, try rolling a ball to him while he's sitting on the floor. In a short time, he will roll it back with a limited degree of accuracy. I see a big difference in the physical abilities of the children I teach if they have played pitch and catch with someone. Simple activities like throwing a ball with your little one help build a confident child who is more likely to attempt more difficult athletic challenges.

If you have the ability to engage in egoless play and have fun with your child without imposing judgment, chapters 6, 7, and 8 will give you a blueprint for how to teach your child. When your child is between four and eight years old, it is important to transition some parental teaching to a certified professional sports dual-goal teacher. This will exponentially accelerate your child's developmental learning process. A child will experience a quicker developmental learning curve through a professional sports dual-goal teacher.

The most basic dual-goal teaching begins with a parent encouraging a child to crawl, then walk, then walk without assistance. Verbal instruction and positive reinforcement should be given every step of the way. Parents are dual-goal teachers when they teach both a physical skill and a verbal communication skill simultaneously.

It's important for parents to teach their child the invaluable lesson of body awareness. That lesson is to know the right side of one's body from the left. Begin by having your child identify his right hand/foot and his left hand/foot. Next, add the eyes and ears. Now add the nose and mouth, to teach the position of "middle" on his face. The next step would be to introduce the concept of up and down by using a child's head and feet.

Verbalizing instructions to your child is important because they are the building blocks for establishing adult vocabulary, which in turn will help with communication skills for a lifetime. It's very helpful in understanding simple directions from point A to point B. Knowing one's left hand/foot from one's right is a prerequisite for learning any physical activity, especially sports. Understanding this concept will aid with many skills, including playing board games, putting shoes on, and following simple directions.

Learning basic body awareness and self-care has an effect on your child's confidence and ability to learn academic and athletic lessons. A four- to eight-year-old child's confidence is affected when he can't find a bathroom at school because he doesn't know what a left or right turn means. Having coached sports for over fifty years, I am astonished at how many six-year-olds and older don't know their left from their right. Children who don't will freeze and stare, like the proverbial deer at night with a bright light shining in its eyes. The deer will actually freeze until the light is redirected away from it. Children do the same thing when facing a challenge and unsure of how to proceed. Children who confuse their right and left frequently react by looking to see what their peers are doing.

Parents have the opportunity to set the foundation for dual-goal teaching long before children go to preschool. Dual-teachable moments happen many times a day. An early start is beneficial to academic and emotional development, compared to a child without the same exposure.

As a parent, stepparent, grandparent, and coach, I know firsthand that there are many challenges in educating and raising children. Even at its best, everyday family life requires a shift in priorities and flexibility in a series of emergencies. These occasions consume much of our emotional energy. One of the ways I suggest dealing with many of the difficulties of parenting is for parents to create a plan or blueprint for how they will handle challenges. I believe in creating a written plan for your child in academics, athletics, and finances. Why have a written plan? These flexible plans, if executed properly, have the potential to shape your child's lifelong goals. If nothing else, they aid in tracking your past thoughts and intentions in parenting. Use the plans as a reference point so that you can go back and review.

Let me not understate the necessity and importance of a financial plan for you and your partner and a separate plan for you to implement with your child. Managing money is one of the greatest gifts a child can be given by her parents. Having savings is the key to future emotional and financial happiness. It seems to me that this generation focuses on gaining possessions, but not on saving money for their future needs.

Money problems can cause, but are not limited to, divorce, separation, frustration, and mistrust in relationships. My mother grew up during the Depression; however, she understood how to handle money. I was surprised to find that several popular media financial advisors convey the same message that I heard from my mom sixty years ago. The keys are:

- Have an income-based budget that guides you to spend less money than you make

- Buy only what you need and not what you may want (what great advice)

- Save part of your income for a time of unemployment, retirement, family education, and vacations

- Enjoy saving for your future more than spending money now on nonessential items (my mom's specialty)

The values of the plans you create are only as good as the systematic manner in which you implement them. Parenting is a journey in which we sometimes get lost. These plans will act as a road map and as a reminder of your intentions in parenting.

It would be remiss of me not to mention other categories of teachers (besides schoolteachers and sports coaches) who have the platform to dual-goal teach your children. Dual-goal teachers who oversee individuals, teams, or clubs—such as debate, chess, yearbook, music, and school newspapers, to name a few activities—all have an opportunity to make a difference in your child's development.

Let me not forget the potential impact of religious teachers who might positively influence your child's development. Exposure to a faith/religion can become a supporting tool in reinforcing parental teachings and can help develop a faith in a power higher than oneself. In my research, I spoke with religious leaders who reported having very little parental support with ongoing access to children after a certain age or after a particular religious milestone has been achieved.

This disconnect seems to be the result of convenient parental choices, such as "does the family want to go to church or go to the beach?" The other issue for parents is that the support that religious groups offer children is not always adequately communicated to them. What a waste of a potentially valuable resource. The exception is in cases where religious groups have state-certified schools for their faithful and others to attend. There are a variety of religious groups and congregations to meet the needs of modern spiritual families. Based on your spiritual vision, you may find a group that benefits your family by offering a sense of community and supporting your values.

Now let us address the very real stigma in sports that is attached to a child winning or losing, and the major effects it has on both the child and the parent. After a child competes, many coaches, and almost every parent, ask the same shaming question, "Did you win?" Early childhood is the best time to give a very useful definition of the word win that can be applied to almost everything a child experiences. Win is a word that creates a most specific impression, and can evoke a warm fuzzy feeling of happiness and pride. If your child did not win, losing could cause embarrassment and shame and feelings of failure. Worst of all, the child may not want to try the sport again. Unfortunately, I often see parents and coaches handle this issue poorly.

When a beginner plays against an advanced beginner or an intermediate player, the beginner will most likely lose. The beginner will be discouraged about the results of the match, and if not properly nurtured, will probably choose to play the Game Boy or Nintendo rather than play sports again.

With a dual-goal teacher, the beginner will learn and practice new skill sets. When that beginner again plays the advanced player and improves her performance, this is winning. And yes, even if the player loses the match, this improvement is what defines winning. It is great to see a child compete, not win the match, and still walk away feeling good about his effort and improvement.

I have asked literally hundreds of children age four to ten years old, "What does winning mean to you?" Unfortunately, they all had virtually the same response. Most said winning means: the champion is well liked and a good person, the best in the world, a special person, makes a lot of money, has nice cars, nice houses, and gets a lot of things for free.

So when a child is asked by his parent, "Did you win?" and the answer is no, what do you think the child thinks of himself? And what does that child think his parent think of him? Is it any wonder that 70 percent of children give up on sports by the age of thirteen?

Certainly, athletic sports being a component of young children's development is not a new concept. In my era, physical education and sports were part of the grammar and high school curriculum. We actually chose teams and played athletic games during recess, after lunch, and after school. I remember having a snack after school and rushing to be the first one outside to play sports. Playing sports was a daily event that was fun and offered a bonding experience with other children. It meant everything to me.

School was something I "had" to do, but I had a true passion for playing sports. Being able to play sports on school teams and at the playground was great motivation to maintain good grades. It gave me a strong sense of belonging, pride, and emotional satisfaction that I found nowhere else.

Let me share an example of sports being used as a platform to teach children life lessons and as a motivational tool for disadvantaged children in overcoming their circumstances. While reading the following story, reflect on what a dual-goal teacher could do for your child.

A great model of children benefiting academically and in other developmental areas from athletic sports is at Arise Academy in New Orleans. This school offers a program called A's and Aces, endorsed by the United States Tennis Association and the National Junior Tennis and Learning Network, which was founded by tennis great Arthur Ashe. This program's mission is to provide academic help, life skills, and tennis instruction to children as a way to increase their opportunities for success.

The school currently consists of kindergarten to fourth grade students and adds a grade level each year. The school teaches typical academic subjects, but, in addition, it offers lessons in vocal and instrumental music as part of its curriculum. Visual and performing arts, technology, and tennis are taught as well.

The A's and Aces curriculum is modeled after the teachings of Arthur Ashe. Children learn about Ashe's belief in himself, his educational achievements, and his strong belief in good nutrition. He also had an impeccable work ethic, and played golf, baseball, and the trombone. Ashe believed that hard work and perseverance were the cornerstones of success. The students learn all about Arthur, presented in an interesting way. Students learn about Ashe's tools for success and what skills they could adopt to serve them as personal tools. They are also encouraged to ask questions and explore how they compare Ashe to other role models. I personally knew Arthur and found him to be one of the kindest and most articulate people I have ever met.

The power of learning through athletics is available to all children, not just children labeled disadvantaged or at risk. And let us not kid ourselves, parents—in today's world, every child is at risk of being led in the wrong direction. Participation in athletic activities can have the most dramatic impact on children's development, with parents dual-goal teaching their children at a very young age.

CHAPTER TWO
Parenting Styles and Observations

In today's world, parents are a unique group who differ in childhood experiences, education, personalities, temperaments, passions, and the way that they approach parenting their children. Parents come in a variety of combinations. Heterosexual and gay couples can be married for the first time, first-time married with a remarried, two remarried, and living together without marriage. Moreover, there are mixed marriages in terms of religions, cultures, and races.

Similarly, children can have different birth circumstances: biological, adopted, birthed by a surrogate mother. Siblings can be biological siblings, stepsiblings, or siblings by adoption or surrogate birth.

You just have to look at the high divorce rate in the United States of 50 percent to understand that difficulties come with marriage and partnership. Add parenting to the mix, and marriage becomes even more difficult, because a couple trying to maintain a connection with each other picks up the added challenge of meeting a child's needs. Those needs often conflict with the couple's needs.

Now, if that is somewhat confusing to us, think about how confusing it could be to children in any of these environments. I am not judging any type of parent, but it's important to recognize the diversity of families so we are reminded that our children's friends may have a home environment very different from our own.

The parenting dilemma can easily be understood. Children do not come with an operation manual, nor are any of us automatically certified to raise our children properly without a lot of support and research. At best, proper parenting is a demanding 24/7 responsibility for most of our lives. Often, parenting styles take the subconscious form of either raising our children in a way absolutely opposite to how we were raised, or in exactly the same way as we were raised.

In parenting my own children and stepchildren, I had as many successes and made as many mistakes as any parent. But according to feedback from my children and stepchildren, much of my parenting was actually quite good. My intention was always to be the best parent I was capable of being. Based on the tools I had at the time, I did the best I could. My shortcoming in my first marriage was that I did not unlearn the negative ways in which I was parented. I was also unaware of other parenting models. I was caught up in my career, and the financial worry of being able to provide for my family.

What helped me in adjusting my parenting was to first understand the traits in my own parents that harmed me. A combination of talking with hundreds of other parents, hindsight, my deep interest in child development, and being a dual-goal coach has helped me formulate specific parenting success factors. The key ingredients in a happy family start with a couple growing together emotionally, staying intimate, and respecting each other.

I now feel very confident in what works and what doesn't. The personality of the child also makes a big difference in parenting. Just because your child comes from your genes doesn't mean your child will be like you! If you expect your child to be like you in personality and temperament, this could cause untold frustrations for both of you.

My dad taught me an important basic parenting skill that I used, with a variation in his approach. But first allow me to tell you a little bit about my dad. He was a brilliant man in math, science, electronics, and teaching. In fact, he was contracted to the navy during WW II and taught the operation and repair of radar. While gifted in many ways, he lacked the ability to provide a safe and nurturing childhood because he insisted on perfection. Both his parents were college graduates. His mother was a grammar school teacher who died when he was twelve years old. His father, because of the era, was forced to work, and he delegated my dad's upbringing to my dad's aunt.

These changes and transitions in his caretakers during formative years marked my dad forever. He lived in an environment that was discriminatory toward him. He felt unwanted, alone, and deserted. As his child, I suffered from his authoritarian style of parenting. And at the same time, I benefited from the many life lessons he taught me.

My dad and I bonded when we made wooden model planes and boats together. The kits were pretty primitive in the 1950s as to fit and detail, but a lot of fun to build. What he taught me was a system for construction, including cutting, sanding, gluing, and sanding the models again. We inspected the model for the correctness of fit for all the pieces and did a survey to ensure all the pieces were in the correct places. The good thing about the wooden models was it was easy to make a part that was either missing or broken during construction out of balsa wood. Then we chose the paint colors and proceeded to paint the model.

What I learned at the age of six was that a good system, if followed, could produce a very fine product. If I deviated from the system, this caused rework and frustration for both of us. I found this was also true in academics. Proper study habits produced good grades. And, of course, the reverse was true. It took me an additional seven years to realize that it was also true in my sports pursuits. This realization happened when I was introduced to my high school track, basketball, and tennis coaches. My skill sets started to improve exponentially because of proper coaching.

Although the way I had been parented was flawed, I had a model of parenting quality control to follow. I learned that how my own children's lives turned out depended on my system of parenting. What I changed from my dad's approach to teaching was to make the process fun; my children did not have to be perfect. The lesson, especially for parents of young children, is that it is OK to "make mistakes." Mistakes are part of the learning process. Unfortunately, my dad did not accept mistakes.

Both my parents were teachers by profession and had a skilled style of explaining many different things to me at a very early age. Even though rules for my behavior involved rigid expectations, there were a lot of teaching, explanation, and life lessons happening as well. The importance of good manners that they instilled in me has been a gift throughout my life in formal, informal, sports, and social settings.

As a young child, I was taught how to plant and grow flowers and vegetables, select food from the grocery store, prepare meals, handle knives, start a fire, wire a lamp, build a radio, perform carpentry, fix a broken pipe, and rethread it. I was taught the appreciation of classical music and had piano lessons. As a family, we rowed boats and chased after the ducks and swans in Audubon and City Park lagoons. We also chased the ducks with the radio-controlled model boats that we built together while sitting on the shoreline of the lagoons.

When I was ten years old, my dad and I built a motorized go-cart with an engine from an old washing machine, wheels from a wagon, and a frame we made out of wood. It featured a lever that pressed against the back wheels for brakes and another lever that engaged the pulleys on the engine and rear axle to go forward only. I thought that was quite cool. At the age of fourteen, I helped my dad rebuild a 1952 Renault. We spent months doing bodywork, rebuilding the engine, installing a new wiring harness and brakes, and painting the car.

I did not know at the time how much all these projects would influence my life today. Yesterday I fixed the wiring in one of my lamps and then looked up to my dad, who passed away in 2006, and thanked him. I do not worry about having my cars fixed because when something goes wrong, I know that 99 percent of the time I can fix it. More importantly, I know what a mechanic needs to do to fix it. I enjoy replacing locks and working on my mechanical clocks. I have an appreciation for the depth of knowledge I gained in many subjects that I was exposed to by both my parents.

Many weekends were spent in the country, riding horses, chasing chickens, and playing with an endless array of animals and neighboring farm children. I particularly enjoyed riding bareback and shooting my pellet pistol at tin cans on fence posts. Later in life, I used my riding skills to play polo for the Hilton Head Polo Club in South Carolina. A highlight of my childhood was the family meals with my aunts, uncles, and cousins. We all had a chance to talk, listen, tease, and reminisce with one another.

Summer vacations were always fun, and a continual flow of life lessons and opportunities to discuss nature, science, and different cultures was presented some sixty years ago. I will never forget the time we were driving through a very rural farming area in the state of Mississippi and I commented about the poor people living in literal shacks alongside the road. The scene was of families on their front porches with many children playing in the sprawling front yards so close to the highway.

That image is still fresh in my mind today. I can see the rope swings with no seats tied to tree branches.

There were no slides, monkey bars, or swing sets like at the playground near where I lived. I thought they were missing out on something. My parents reminded me that I enjoyed sliding down the levee next to the Mississippi River on a modified cardboard box for a sled. And they cited the industriousness of those parents who made their children's playground. I began to have an appreciation for people whose environment or culture was different from mine.

My parents also pointed out that the people were not necessarily poor in happiness, love, or a strong-valued family life, just poor to me because of the dwelling in which they lived. What a lame way to judge people! They added that those people might own their house with hundreds of acres of land outright and not have a mortgage like we had. In fact, they said that a house is not a measure of the financial or emotional wealth of a family.

My father's French roots influenced much of my childhood. The French are known historically for sharing the realities of life with children at a very early age. In recent years, the French parenting style has evolved to become more Americanized. From my father's traditional French style of parenting, I learned to be patient and respectful at the age of three or four years old I learned the meaning of family values, respect, and spending time with extended family on weekends for meals. As I got a little older, I was afraid of angering my dad. Fortunately, my dad traveled often for work and my mother gave me most of the nurturing that every child needs.

We cannot relive or change the past, nor as adults blame our parents for our actions or current predicaments. I took full responsibility for myself and drastically changed the path I was following. This insight that I have now on unhealthy parenting is simple. No matter what seemingly good intention a parent brings to the family, if it affects a child negatively, it has to be dealt with ASAP. Although my dad's projects with me and his life lessons proved valuable, I suffered because he was not a very loving and caring father.

My mother was consistently attentive, loving, and nurturing. She spent most of her time protecting me from the wrath of my dad. He was verbally abusive to my mother and me. What really bothered me was his physical abuse of my mother. This behavior lasted until his death. He was an alcoholic, with all the traits of drastic mood and personality changes. As high as his upside was, his downside was hell. By that I mean that none of the neighbors saw or knew what my mother and I experienced. But all our relatives on both sides knew of my dad's temper. At the time, in the 1950s and 1960s, his alcoholism was not recognized because he did not go to bars or drink during the week.

My mother stayed with him and endured his behavior because of her religious beliefs. She also had worked so hard for their house and feared that she would be left homeless if she divorced him. In other areas, she was a very strong individual. I am proud to say that, while teaching at a grammar school, she started college at the age of thirty-eight and graduated six years later.

Because I had experienced the extreme unpleasantness of being raised in a volatile environment and had few tools to understand marriage, I decided in my adolescence that I would not be trapped in a marriage that did not work. Unlike my mother, I would just get a divorce. This type of thinking showed my compulsive and immature nature at that time, and for many years after. That, along with my dependence on thinking that other people could make me happy, resulted in a revolving door of marriages. I remarried sixteen years after my first marriage ended. My next marriages were a disaster financially and emotionally for me. I was starting to realize that I was the key to my happiness, not other people.

I entered a fourth marriage. The person was first a friend, and still is today. In a mature way, we acknowledged our similarities and differences and divorced. In fact, I recently had lunch with her and my former stepchildren. I learned that I had actually done a very good job as a stepfather. Their opinion of the seven years that we were together as a family was quite flattering. The stepchildren are now in their mid-twenties and are fine adults. I have lived the role of a stepparent with the experience of having been a birth parent.

What I learned as a stepparent was that I could have the same sense of parental love and responsibility toward my stepchildren that I had with my own children. More importantly, I realized the impact that a stepparent has on the lives of stepchildren. As a stepparent in marriage number four, I thought I was just a "fill-in" because their dad was always part of their life. However, this is not the case; stepparents play an important role in the outcome of their stepchildren's lives. Luckily, my own children were mature and old enough to realize that I always had their best interest at heart.

The trauma of divorce throws everyone's life into turbulence. It is a nightmare at best for any child who experiences the negative environment caused by separation and the changes as a result of divorce. Where do children experiencing divorce get their needed nurturing during this stressful period? Too often, parents spend their time retaliating against each other and the child becomes a pawn in the aftermath of a failed marriage.

The pettiness and ploys used to hurt the other parent during and after a divorce are often criminal. Under the label of being the "best thing for everyone," divorce inevitably creates turbulence and stress for a child. It reaches its highest flash point when the divorced couple begins new relationships with other people. This sets the stage for four adults agreeing only not to agree about anything. Sadly, the one who bears the brunt of the drama are the children, who are left feeling insecure and unloved.

I know from personal experience the traumatic effects divorce and the drama between previously married couples and future relationships can have on a child. I coach hundreds of children with divorced parents, and they exhibit the devastating pain and long-lasting effects of a combative divorce. I witness weekly the crippling effects upon wonderful children because of the gamesmanship of some parents.

Divorce is not always a negative path with ill side effects for a family. In fact, divorce in many instances may be the best alternative for all involved. It is important to note that, in my opinion, professional counseling is mandatory for each individual separately and as a couple. Counseling should not be used as a last resort in marriage. It should be used to work out problems that are of concern as soon as it is obvious that the couple cannot solve the issues. This has saved many marriages. Also, without the proper counseling, the tendency for the individuals involved is to bring their "negative stuff" to their next relationship. Some key ingredients for a possible successful divorce are:

- Both parents admitting their responsibility in the failed marriage

- Both parents agreeing the divorce is best for each of them

- Both parents wanting the best for their offspring

- Both parents wanting the best for each other's future

- Both parents seeking professional counseling for themselves and their children

- Both parents being comfortable with themselves and on their own before seeking another mate

The ironic thing to me is that if several of the bullet points above were practiced in marriage, divorce would not be needed.

Although my parents never divorced, I personally suffered from some of the same issues that children in divorced situations face. Their unhealthy union left me feeling protective of my mother and angry toward my father. My point is that if the marriage is not working for the parents, it certainly is not working for the children. And if that is the case, after both work with a marriage counselor, an amicable divorce maybe best for everyone.

The correlation between my life experiences, including several marriage situations, and my passion to be a dual-goal coach is quite simple. I understand the difficulty of parenting from a parent's and a stepparent's perspective. But more importantly, I know how difficult it is for a child, even in the best of home environments, to feel truly safe, secure, and loved. I believe that, as a dual-goal coach, I am able to give the reinforcement of positive experiences to a child's life that builds self-confidence and character. It takes a team of positive role models starting at an early age to support and create positive experiences. As a product of a dysfunctional home environment myself, I want to make a difference to both parents and their children by sharing my observations.

The bottom line in parenting is to ensure that the foundation for our child's self-esteem is developed in his/her early childhood. For that to occur, the environment we create has to be safe and allow children to trust and value themselves.

The following are parenting styles that I have observed: authoritative, authoritarian, Chinese, permissive, uninvolved, helicopter, and immigrant. There is also a mix of the styles that overlap, which parents choose based on the styles' success in producing the desired outcomes. The immigrant style will not be found in any resource material since it is a style that I coined. If you have known many immigrants firsthand, you will detect their parenting style easily.

Authoritative style:
The authoritative parenting style establishes rules and guidelines that the parents expect their child to follow. Their discipline is more supportive for the outcome of the child being self-regulated. These parents tend to be understanding and nurturing as opposed to immediately punishing. They also tweak the rules or guidelines if they are unjust to the child or parent. They teach their child to be flexible in decision making. The basic outcome of this style is a child who is successful, happy, and capable.

Authoritarian style:
The authoritarian parenting style that my dad used has strict, unbendable rules and changing guidelines that parents expect to be followed by their child. Not following any of the rules is grounds for punishment. To add insult to injury, if the same rule is broken twice, the punishment might be doubled.

This parenting style lacks an explanation of how the rules were derived. The only explanation is usually "because I said so." This is said to the child often. It is an uncomfortable style in a family setting as well as in the workplace.

The outcome of this style is generally a child who is extremely proficient and obedient. However, his/her self-esteem, social skills, and happiness levels are very low. My observation has been that it is often easy to have an insight into a person's childhood simply by examining how he/she behaves and relates to others as an adult.

Chinese style:
The Chinese parenting style is more of a cultural style and very close to the authoritarian style. The Chinese style is documented rather well in the book Battle Hymn of the Tiger Mom, penned by Amy Chua. Amy is a mother who subjected her children to an obsessive, almost abusive

level of pressure in pursuit of superlative achievement, not only in school but also in music. Her children were expected always to be "the best." They had to practice the piano or violin three to four hours a day, seven days a week. Because of major conflicts with her children, Chua eventually chose to change her parenting style in the best interest of her children, despite her deep cultural roots. Different cultures lead to different parenting styles.

Permissive style:
The permissive parenting style is one where parents make few demands of their child. They are lenient, avoid confrontation, and tend to be their child's friend rather than parent. The result of this style is a child who has low achievement in school, experiences problems with authority, and has very low levels of self-regulation and happiness.

Uninvolved style:
The uninvolved parenting style is one of poor communication, few rules, and responsiveness actions that are slow to none. Their child's needs are only basically met, and in fact are often neglected or rejected. And the parents are often detached from their child. Across the board, this style creates a child who has very low self-esteem, a major lack of self-control, and who is not as competent as his/her peers.

Immigrant style:
The immigrant parenting style seems to be a mix of the authoritarian and authoritative styles. Firstborn immigrant children in America seem to have a distinct advantage over American-born second-, third-, and fourth-generation children. In my opinion, this is because of their parents' superior work ethic. Because of their high level of work ethic, sacrifice, and opportunism for their children's future, their children truly appreciate them.

These children do not have a sense of entitlement, which is quite refreshing. Their family loyalty is placed above popularity with peers. And more importantly, they seem more appreciative of their education, work, and financial opportunities.

Helicopter style:
The helicopter parenting style is attributed to parents with children born in America between 1980 and 2005, called Millennials. You may not have heard the names Millennials or helicopter parents, but they are easily recognizable. Helicopter parents do not let their child experience failure in anything. All activities are geared to fail-proof their child. This leads the child not to know how to handle failure even as an adult. They also treat their children like they are very special. This creates a myth for the child that he/she can do anything without consequences for his/her actions. Millennials are also called the trophy generation. No matter what sport or activity the child is in, the entire team or group gets a trophy or award, for just being on the team.

This begs the question, when do these children learn to handle failure? Failure is one issue that does have grave consequences if not properly addressed with the guidance of knowledgeable parents. My neighbor's brother teaches management classes for many high-profile companies, to help these gifted Millennials. A cottage industry has sprung up based on a generation of people who can't handle failure.

During the last eight years, young children have often asked me if they will get an award after a lesson or when a session ends. Early on, I was so taken aback by this question that my only response was, "There is no trophy or award!" And I thought to myself, Why do they want something special for just showing up? Aren't they having fun playing tennis? Then I had an epiphany. Either their parents were bribing them to do things with gifts, or they had played in a "feel-good" sport setting where all participants receive awards and the game score is not kept so that everyone is a winner. After some research, I found that both things were happening with many children.

However, I now have an antidote for the children's request for awards. Knowing that most children have visited a Disney theme park, I ask if they got an award for doing so. Of course they say no. Then I ask them what they liked about Disney. The answers are always that they had fun and it made them feel good. I then ask if they have fun during my tennis lessons and they reply, yes! So I conclude with them that both visiting Disney and my lessons are fun and do not need an award. They always agree that they do have fun in my lesson and do not need another reward. Having fun is the reward.

Developing a parenting philosophy for your child starts with a parenting business plan. Yes, you and your partner are in the parenting business. In a perfect world it would be discussed before the birth of your child, rather than after your child has made her debut. The plan starts with a mission statement.

The mission statement should be a parent joint effort with important issues highlighted, such as to focus on the academic, social, emotional, cognitive, and physical developmental needs. The areas of finance, health, and family values need to be in that plan, too. Parents must take every opportunity to teach life lessons, and being jointly responsible, they should be guided by a fluid written plan and budget. The bottom line is to nurture a happy, healthy, and well-educated child who transitions into a happy and self-sufficient adult.

Another ingredient in the mission statement is the importance of happiness for both you and your spouse. If the parents are not growing as individuals, as a couple, and as a family, it is a major distraction for all concerned. Marriage without a child is a work in progress. Add the dynamics of a child, and it is a much more difficult challenge, especially since parenting causes changes in priorities for both parents.

In my eyes, the key ingredient in any family starts with the relationship of the parents. The lack of keeping emotional and sexual intimacy alive must be worked on daily. It is easy to be caught up in putting your child first and neglecting each other. So keep that spark alive that originally brought the two of you together. Concentrate on the positives of each other, not the negatives. To grow with and enjoy each other is difficult and often overlooked by parents.

Learn to have adult fun together and often. And yes, spend time together without your child. Sharing a phone call or text during the day connects you with your spouse in an ongoing way. Work out together. And when you need to be quiet or alone, don't hesitate to tell your spouse. I didn't feel the need to be emotionally intimate with my former female partners, but now I understand the importance of this connection. I see the difference it makes in my current unparalleled relationship.

An emotionally happy couple will be better prepared to parent their child and create a healthy environment. That was definitely missing in my childhood. And it is not too late to improve your relationship with your spouse for your family's growth and happiness.

In your written plan for your child, set goals for his/her development based on age, your budget, his/her personality type, and individual abilities. Your child's preferred learning style should also be considered. A child may be a visual learner by sight, an auditory learner by listening, or a kinesthetic learner by touching, doing, or moving. And note that genetic siblings will most likely have different learning style preferences.

There is no perfect plan for being perfect parents. Continually explore new ways to become a better parent. Learn every tool you can to help in your quest to do the best for your child. Remember that your parenting will create lifetime memories, habits, and preferences for your child.

From personal experience, the greatest tool for parenting is not as much to learn how to parent, but rather to unlearn what you already know. Most people who experience difficulty in parenting go back to what they know, which are the dynamics from their family of origin. It is like trying to do something the same way all the time and expecting a different outcome. Relying on past experience limits our ability to grow and problem solve effectively. This is why a particular parenting style often persists through many generations.

The best role model for a child is a happy parent who's comfortable and secure with himself. This leads to a secure and comfortable environment for your entire family. If you are stressed out most of the time, the environment that you create will produce anxiety for your loved ones.

Employ lateral thinking to restructure the "whys" and "what ifs" and allow you to experience other ways of accomplishing goals. This approach has helped me in all aspects of my life. It has also helped people like Albert Einstein, Bill Gates, Steve Jobs, or Galliano think "out of the box."

Being a happy individual is not to frustrate yourself by always looking back on missed opportunities or poor choices in your life. Know that things can be a lot better, and do not strangle yourself with past mistakes. Although I have made more than my share of mistakes in life, I am very happy now with 99 percent of my relationships, and 100 percent happy working with children.
Some parenting tips to consider:

- Use your child's missteps as a teaching tool.

- Catch and comment on the good things your child does.

- Be an inquisitive and investigative parent.

- Be consistent in your actions toward your child.

- Children experience stress, too, so help them cope with it.

- Reducing your personal stress will benefit your child.

- Teach manners as well as caring and respectful behavior.

- Have an engaging mealtime routine for all the family.

- Seek change through insight and questioning.

- Parents need downtime to recharge themselves.

- Let children make mistakes in order to learn from them.

- Look for teachable moments daily with your child.

- Parent as a team, and not "good cop/bad cop."

- Enjoy your children during your parenting journey.

- Work on your marriage daily and stay in love.

Hopefully, a tip or two will be helpful to you and your partner.

CHAPTER THREE
Nutrition for Mental and Physical Health Benefits

———

As a parent, grandparent, and dual-goal coach, I know firsthand how tough it is to help kids stick to a healthy diet. It's not easy, but ultimately, parents are responsible for their child's eating habits. It's not the responsibility of your child's school, nanny, sitter, or grandparent. Your child isn't capable of making responsible food choices. Having a child choose his food would be like asking the fox to close the door to the henhouse!

As parents, we all think we understand the importance of a proper diet, yet I discover daily that 35–85 percent of the children I coach don't have good eating habits. I don't know if we realize the short- and long-term effects. I frequently ask my students to tell me what they ate for breakfast, lunch, or dinner. They will say, "I did not eat anything," or "We had a hamburger and fries in the car," but very seldom do I hear, "We had some vegetables and chicken/fish."

When I witness children in a morning class who act abnormally sluggish or irritable, or who lack focus, I want to uncover the root cause of the behavior. I want to know if it is a lack of interest in learning tennis, poor nutrition, or a distraction not related to their lesson. My goal is to teach tennis and to help them overcome whatever challenges they may face.

The deficiencies in breakfast diets range from a child eating a doughnut or a piece of cold pizza to not eating anything. Interestingly, some children will defend their parents who fail to provide breakfast. Children defensively say their parents were too busy, ran out of time, or there was no food in the house. Should parents be faulted if they run out of food, causing their child not to have a healthy start for the day? Clearly, it is not the young child's responsibility.

In early afternoon lessons, I notice a greater percentage of children with poor eating habits. The greater numbers in the afternoon are a result of some poor breakfast habits, poor lunch habits, plus an improper snack before after-school activities. Children will tell me, "I did not eat all my lunch," or "I traded my packed lunch for a friend's lunch of chips, cookies, and a candy bar," or "My parents ran out of our healthy food and packed this lunch for me instead," or "I played during lunch and threw my food away so my mom would think I ate lunch."

The parents of children who say that they did not eat breakfast usually disappear quickly from the court area where I teach tennis. Sadly, it's often the same children who continually seem to have an unhealthy diet. In fact, a small percentage of children seem to be convinced that breakfast is not important. Where do you think they got this idea? I find that nutrition during the school year is much better than during the summer vacation months due to the scheduling of meals. Good nutrition doesn't need a vacation! Nutritional meal structure is difficult to keep in place without distractions, much less with a lapse of two to three months.

Consider what is at stake, short and long term, for your child based on dietary choices. Young children need the proper foods for bone, organ, and brain development. As they become teenagers and young adults, nutrition remains vitally important. An early start in healthy eating sets the stage for lifetime habits.

THE GOOD: What Is Good Nutrition?

If we examine the nations that are the healthiest, without as much chronic disease and with maintenance of a healthy weight, we will notice that their diets are based on plants in the most natural state. The population doesn't eat processed or enhanced food. Food in its natural state contains all the vitamins, minerals, and energy that we need. If the food (most often in a package) is enhanced, it means that it has been processed first, and in many cases stripped of the healthy nutrients.

For the sake of everyone's health, it makes a lot of sense to focus on making good nutritional choices. Almost everybody (and you probably know somebody in your circle of family and friends who is included in that group) will get heart disease, diabetes, cancer, or other chronic disease in his/her lifetime. The risk of developing diabetes, coronary artery disease, certain cancers, and other chronic illnesses can be drastically reduced through proper nutrition. Give your child the gift of proper nutrition. Put the seeds of healthy choices in his/her mind now, and your child will thank you later. And remember that you must be an example to your child by making good food choices.

The main rule of healthy nutrition is that you must center the food on your plate and your child's plate around starches—adding flavor, color, and variety with non-starchy vegetables and fruits. It's very simple.

Starches to eat: whole grains, legumes, and starchy vegetables, such as barley, brown rice, wheat, rye, oats, spelt, etc. Also products made from these grains, such as tortillas, pasta, breads, and whole grain cereals.

Legumes include dried beans, lentils, and peas. There are many variations of beans: adzuki, black, white, cannellini, chickpeas, kidney, lima, navy, pinto, soy, and more.

Starchy vegetables include potatoes, yams, sweet potatoes, winter squash, etc.

Non-starchy vegetables: green leafy vegetables, such as kale, chard, spinach, collards, mustard greens. Other vegetables such as zucchini, carrots, beets, radishes, jicama, onions, garlic, fennel, snow peas, mushrooms, broccoli, cauliflower, asparagus, celery, brussels sprouts.

Fruits: citrus fruits (lemons, oranges, limes), berries (blueberries, blackberries, raspberries, cranberries), apples, pears, peaches, plums, cherries, mangoes, melons, and many more.

As you can see, there are such a variety of foods we can and should eat.

For things that we should not eat, there are two approaches:

1) For maximum health, well-being and performance, avoid meat, poultry, dairy, eggs, animal fats, oils, and everything processed. This may sound like a very radical approach, and not everybody is ready to take this step. It's OK if you don't, but it is good to be aware of it.

2) If you choose to eat meat and dairy, always select unprocessed, low-fat variations, preferably organic, without added hormones. The majority of the food on your plate should be starches, vegetables, and fruits, while meat and dairy should be just a small addition.

THE BAD: What to Avoid?

Encourage your children to stay away from polyunsaturated fats, which can cause inflammatory responses in brain tissue and foster blood damage. High concentrations of polyunsaturated oils can be found in safflower, sunflower, and corn oils. They also impede blood flow and are harmful to blood vessels. So, where are these oils commonly used? The oils are found in many processed foods, such as TV dinners, boxed cakes, microwave popcorn, fries, doughnuts, most margarines, etc. Other things to avoid are high fructose corn syrup, which has been linked to obesity. Food additives and colorings are found in many snacks in which you don't expect them, and these chemicals have been linked to Attention Deficit Hyperactive Disorder (ADHD). Kids who frequently consume soft drink and sports nutrition drinks, which are high in sugar, have more cavities and are at greater risk for obesity and diabetes. Keep the nutrition simple and natural.

A new study released in February 2013, by D. Robert H. Lustig, author of Fat Chance, reveals that the effects of sugar are worse than originally thought. Conclusive proof shows that sugar is the causation of diabetes worldwide and is responsible for obesity, high blood pressure, type 2 diabetes, and liver disease. One-third of our daily intake comes from sweetened juices, sports drinks, and soft drinks. A sixth comes from desserts, candy, and ice cream. The other 50 percent comes from processed foods such as salad dressings, barbecue sauce, hamburger buns, hamburger meat, and tomato sauce.

It is so tempting to reward your children with candy, soft drinks, and fast foods. I see this happen almost every time I shop at a grocery store. Food as a bribe! Children want candy, ice cream, and other unhealthy snacks. Children ask for these snacks, because they see them advertised on TV and the packaging is so inviting. Usually a parent's first response is no, but after some tears or lobbying by the child, many parents give in. That strategy of rewarding is self-defeating. You are sending the wrong message when you reward a child with something that is unhealthy. This message is counterproductive, and young children do not understand the concept of moderation. We should not reward children for something they should be doing, especially with unhealthy snacks. Remember, you are not their friend first; you are their parent first. Oftentimes, it's not about a child's self-control but about the parent's.

My experience and research have proven that parents play the biggest role in shaping their children's eating habits for a lifetime. It is the parents' responsibility: give children proper foods and teach them at a very early age how to care for their bodies by fueling them with healthy foods.

It's difficult to encourage your child to choose the right foods when you don't encourage healthy eating habits from birth or if you're eating foods you wouldn't serve your child. When you eat something different from your child, this sends a mixed message. You don't want your children to think that, when they are older, it will be OK for them to consume unhealthy foods. I am amazed that many parents don't seem to realize that children are very intelligent little sponges. They recognize double standards at a very young age. Parents are role models in not only eating, but everything that a child witnesses.

THE UGLY: Stay Away
You could never imagine that your child will grow up to do drugs. However, the drug use among children and teens is a stark reality. In big cities or small towns, all ages, races, and sexes, rich or poor, they use drugs. Educate yourself on drugs—which drugs are available, what they can do, and how they can affect one's health.

The first drug introduced to young children is smoking cigarettes. Children, and often adults, do not always view cigarettes as a drug. Each year about five hundred thousand people in the United States alone die from illnesses related to tobacco use. The American Cancer Society cites that smoking cigarettes kills more Americans that alcohol, car accidents, suicide, AIDS, homicide, and illegal drugs combined.

The most popular drugs are amphetamines, cocaine and crack, depressants, ecstasy (Molly), GHB, heroin, inhalants, ketamine, LSD, marijuana, methamphetamines (meth), nicotine, Rohypnol, etc. The most important step for you is to have a talk with your child and educate her on the dangers of drugs. Talk to your child early and often—this is a message worth repeating and reinforcing.

What Is Healthy for My Child?
It is well documented that a particular substance in food is especially good for young children's brain development: antioxidants. These are found in blueberries, raspberries, cherries, prunes, grapes, apples, raisins, and spinach. In adults, antioxidants may reverse deteriorated conditions such as memory loss, motor balance, and complex coordination. Giving your children healthy brain-boosting foods has lifelong benefits.

Children also need adequate amounts of protein to build muscle and grow. The amount of protein needed daily is based on a child's body weight and includes age-related adjustments. Balanced nutrition based on vegetables, fruits, legumes, and grains will supply all the daily protein necessary. In the past, standard advice was to consume two glasses of milk, a peanut butter sandwich, or lean chicken or fish. However, today's nutritionists say that balanced nutrition is based on vegetables, fruits, legumes, and grains. Always choose unprocessed versions of carbohydrates, like full grain cereals, oatmeal, bread, rice, pasta, sweet potatoes, fruits, and vegetables. Avoid supplements, and try to have your child receive proper nutrition from his/her daily meals.

Foods with omega-3 fatty acids improve general brain function and restore memory. Foods high in omega-3 are most cold-water fish such as salmon, sardines, mackerel, and herring, as well as flax oil, walnuts, and almonds. If possible, avoid farm-raised fish, which has higher levels of toxins and antibiotics. Wild-caught fish tend to have more good nutrients, such as omega-3 fatty acids and protein, while being free of antibiotics and pesticides.

So, what should you be feeding your child? We all probably still consider the food pyramid to be the holy grail of advice on nutrition. But recently, the USDA changed it to a new symbol. It's no longer a pyramid but a colorful plate with four sections, representing vegetables, fruits, grains, and protein, plus a side order of dairy. The most important theme of the new "plate" is that fruits and vegetables take up half the plate, with the vegetable portion being slightly larger than the fruit section. The plate has been divided so that the grain section is bigger than the protein section. Nutrition experts recommend eating more vegetables than fruit and more grains than proteins. The future's plate will be filled with plant starches, vegetables, and fruits, with no meat, fish, or dairy. It will be a long process before this will change in the system, but you are encouraged to slowly transition, as this will benefit your child's long-term health and reduce the possibility of developing chronic diseases that are already present in half of the child population!

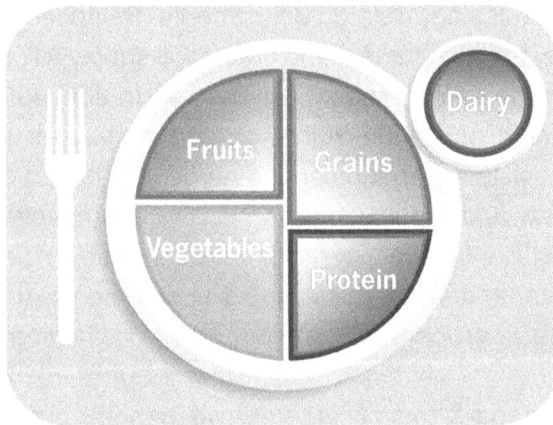

USDA's New Healthy Food Symbol

Along with a proper diet, a child needs thirty minutes of aerobic exercise every day. Chapters 6, 7, and 8 will help you teach your child how to exercise at a very early age.

Your child needs three meals a day and a few nutritious snacks. Limit, or preferably exclude completely, the consumption of processed, high-sugar and high-fat foods, and encourage him to eat fruits, vegetables, whole grains, quinoa, nuts, and sources of lean protein such as legumes. Experts agree that a diet that has plenty of variety and is as natural as possible is best. Discourage foods that are processed and have additives and chemicals. These healthy practices will prevent many medical problems, including obesity, diabetes, developing weak bones, and heart disease.

Don't forget about water. Encourage your child to drink plenty of water, and limit the intake of juice and drinks that contain sugar. I always say, "Bring your racket, a good attitude, and a bottle of water." It's so important for parents to send enough water for the entire session. There's nothing worse than a dehydrated child who is lacking energy and focus.

Modern Warnings`
Most people consider microwaving foods to be safe, but is it? Certainly, microwaves provide modern convenience, especially for busy families who need to quickly prepare kids' meals and snacks. However, many health experts believe that the radiation from microwave ovens causes food molecules to form new molecules called radiolytic compounds. These are mutations that are unknown in the natural world. Ordinary cooking also causes the formation of some radiolytic compounds (which is why eating raw food is so healthy), but microwave cooking may cause them in much higher concentrations. These unnatural compounds are thought to cause deterioration in the blood and immune system. Yes, the microwave is convenient, but it really takes only a few

minutes longer to heat something on the stove or in the oven, and the health benefits may be tremendous.

Are organic foods truly healthier? The word organic refers to the way farmers grow and process agricultural products, such as fruits, vegetables, grains, dairy items, and meat. Organic farming practices encourage soil and water conservation and reduce pollution. In order for food to be labeled "USDA Organic," it must be free of synthetic substances, contain no antibiotics or hormones, and be raised without the use of most conventional pesticides and genetically modified ingredients. Generally speaking, the benefits of buying organic vary greatly depending on what you are buying. And more importantly, organic does not mean "local." It doesn't matter if your apple comes from the local farm or from Japan. As long as it meets USDA standards, it's organic. If buying all organic isn't a priority or financially possible for you, consider buying organic specifically when you're selecting foods that are most heavily contaminated with pesticide and insecticide residues. Examples of these foods include: meat, dairy products, eggs, coffee, peaches, potatoes, peppers, leafy greens such as kale, collards, and spinach, baby food, and anything you eat a lot of or every day. Experts say anything you eat in large quantities should be organic in order to avoid overexposure to certain chemicals.

Buy your nonorganic foods at the local markets. Often, the farmers care more about their produce and environment and don't use pesticides. Choose produce that is in season. It tastes better and the prices are extremely affordable. You can find many websites that offer affordable organic legumes, grains, and other foods.

There are concerns about the health effects of genetically modified foods, better known as GMOs. Chemists and engineers have modified the DNA of foods to make them grow faster and resist disease. The process takes desirable DNA and splits it, with less DNA to improve the less desirable and nutritious DNA. Commercialization of GMO food started in the United States in 1994 with tomatoes engineered to have a longer shelf life and, unlike non-GMO tomatoes, not be ruined by freezing in cold spells.

Since then, strawberries and many other fruits have been modified. And advances in biotechnology have produced crops that resist insects, disease, and weed killers. However, the concern is that the GMOs not only are not as nutritious as the original food but also may be unhealthy.

An article published in the April 2013, issue of the scientific journal Entropy cited that glyphosate, the main ingredient in Roundup, has been found in food that had been sprayed with the weed killer. The popular herbicide could be linked to a range of health problems and diseases, including cancers, infertility, and Parkinson's disease. The study states that, "The negative impact on the body is insidious and manifests slowly over time as inflammation damages cellular systems throughout the body."

The change in the DNA in fruits, vegetables, and farm-raised salmon has concerned many doctors and research scientists, and slowly the general public is increasing its awareness of the issue. In fact, six European countries have banned the use of GMOs. The concern is that the modifications to our foods reduce the nutritional value and may actually harm us. Many of the GMOs are in corn and other foods that are fed to our livestock and other food sources. It is a complicated issue, but I would be remiss in not mentioning the pending time bomb in our food supply.

Do your due diligence, find your sources, and decide that you will consciously care about your child's health. The way your child eats now will shape her future health and well-being.

CHAPTER FOUR
Important Life Lessons for Children

———

Parents and dual-goal sports teachers have many teachable moments that offer children valuable life lessons. I'm passionate about these life lessons that I have chosen, because they go straight to the core of a child being happy and well adjusted for his/her lifetime. Also important is the effect these have on the parents and on the child's ability to function in society.

Life Lesson of Morality
At an early age, children should learn the consequences of their actions and be offered important lessons relating to morality (right and wrong). Teachable moments for me as a coach occur both in my tennis lesson plans and opportunities that I recognize during a class. For parents, it is often the first life lesson taught. Acting on the right thing to do and knowingly avoiding the wrong things is a great compass for a lifetime. In this life lesson, parents must be great role models for the lesson to be followed by their child.

Life Lesson of Coping with Failure
As mentioned before, handling failure is one of the most important life lessons that you can teach to young children. It enables them to overcome the fear of failure in learning anything new. I always tell my students that it is OK to make mistakes. This seems to relieve the self-imposed fear that we all experience at different times in our lives. Related to failure, is that minimizing their mistakes will help them improve in tennis, schoolwork, and all aspects of their lives. Setting the proper level of expectation is important in relation to failure. Through sports dual-goal teaching, children learn to manage disappointment and cope with failure.

Life Lesson of Respect
The life lesson of respect that I always teach is not to allow anyone in my classes to cut in line. To an adult, it may not seem like a big deal, but it is to the children who are cut in front of. In fact, for them it constitutes bullying. If that behavior of cutting in line is not stopped, the learning environment quickly changes to one of frustration and distraction for the entire class. If cutting in line is not addressed, we are giving tacit approval to the line-cutter to continue bullying. Teaching respect for toys, athletic gear, other's toys, etc., are great lessons to learn.

Life Lesson of Responsibility
Responsibility is a life lesson that is extremely important; however, parents often sabotage it unknowingly. For example, if parents always tie a child's shoes, the child quickly learns to expect his/her parents to do it. This is stimulus and response at its best: shoe untied, parents will tie it. Children become conditioned to believe that if their shoes are untied, a parent or someone else has the responsibility to do it for them. Consequently, children have no interest in tying their shoestrings.

Children and parents may need to be reprogrammed. Parents have the opportunity to practice with the child until the child's hands and brain are up to the task of tying his/her own shoestrings. Some parents avoid the issue by buying their children slip-on or strap-fastening shoes. A child being guided to be responsible at an early age is a gift to both the child and the parent.

Life Lesson of Self-Correction
I require my students from four years old and up to know the mechanics of each tennis stroke and the process of a drill. After they have had adequate time to learn the stroke's mechanics, I tell them that they are responsible for the proper grip, ready position, or the technique we are practicing. If they are not in the correct position to hit a certain stroke, I stand still and shrug my shoulders until they remember the correct position. By shrugging my shoulders, I am also teaching children to read the subtleties of body language and how to respond to nonverbal communication. It's amazing what a child can do if properly trained. Of course, I know that parents are aware of how to assist their child in this area, but there often is not enough time to teach this lesson regularly in our fast-paced lives.

Life Lesson of Self-Control
Control of self is another life lesson that I teach to all students, but I tailor each lesson differently to match the personality and behavior of the individual. I introduce the subject by addressing the strategy of controlling the placement of the ball to win points. Most children can figure out where to hit the ball to gain an advantage at almost any point, especially if they know how to play chess. The challenge for a child is to be able to hit the ball in the direction in which she wants it to go. There are two important factors in controlling the ball properly. The mechanics of the stroke and the child's control of emotions are key. I stress the importance of their expectations and controlling their temper in failure. If you aren't able to control your own emotions, you won't be able to control the ball. When a child loses control emotionally, I call it a "junior moment," and encourage the child to acknowledge that it has occurred. Only after a child knows he loses control can he begin to manage those moments of lost self-control.

Life Lesson of Self-Correction
Self-correction is center stage during all lessons when children make a mistake in hitting the ball over the net or missing the intended target. They are taught the basic fundamentals of a stroke, and when they do not hit their target or they hit the ball into the net, I ask them what went wrong. After they understand the mechanics of a stroke, I try to equip my students with the tools of reasoning to identify what may have gone wrong with their mechanics. As they mature, I expect them to identify and correct the problem. I explain that they must take responsibility for their own self-correction because they won't have me to talk to during a match. The goal is for them to be able to reason and solve problems on their own.

Life Lesson of Change and Decision Making
I teach children to expect change and make smart decisions through a game called Bandit. It is a great tool to help overcome the RC (Resistance to Change) factor. It takes three or more students to play and has the components of simple rules, quick decision making, running short distances, exposure to failure, and making decisions that lead to success.

The setup for the game is the players stand in a circle of equal distance from one another, with their racquets on the ground next to them. A racquet is placed in the middle of the circle with the number of balls on the racquet strings that corresponds to the number of children playing the game. At that point, after checking the distances to the racquet and the distances between each player to make it fair, they are ready to play.

The object of the game is to run to the racquet in the middle and take one ball, then run and put that ball on their racquet strings. Next, they run to someone else's racquet and steal that person's ball, and return to their racquet to hopefully be the first to have two balls on their strings.

The rules are:

- With the players standing next to their racquets, the game starts when you say "go"

- Players can have only one ball in their possession at any time

- Players cannot guard or prevent someone from taking a ball off their racquet strings

- Players cannot push or shove anyone

- The winner is the first player to have two balls on his/her racquet strings

After they have mastered the concept of the game, I begin reducing the number of balls on the middle racquet at the start of each successive game. Sometimes I add a ball during the game. The kids love this game. What a great, lasting lesson it teaches them. Being able to comfortably cope with changes serves them well when they start athletic competition and throughout their everyday lives. Let me add that you don't need racquets to play this game paper plates will suffice.

Life Lesson of Consensus

I teach consensus skills by staging a class into two teams and asking the members to choose a name for their teams. I facilitate communication in both teams, giving them guidelines for the conversation. Depending on the age and personality of each child, the process continues to evolve. After a discussion where all have the opportunity to express an opinion, they vote on a team name. The lesson has to be repeated often for the children, especially four- to seven-year-olds, to build consensus skills. This lesson is important because it teaches children the importance of accepting the opinions of others and compromise in making a decision.

Life Lesson of Self-Perception
On my platform as a coach, I am disheartened to find the abundantly growing number of children ages four to ten who state how exceptionally good they are in a sport, and even at playing chess. Especially in summer tennis camp, parents will introduce me to their child and say how good he/she plays. Invariably, their child tells me that he/she is a very good player as well. Ninety-nine percent of the time, the child can't hit a ball.

The problem, in my opinion, is typical of a "helicopter parent." By that I refer to parents who, in an effort to elevate their child's self-esteem or protect them from failure, spin dialogue to make the child actually believe that he/she is very good. Then, when the lesson begins, the child either blames his/her inability to hit a ball on the teacher or gets frustrated with tennis and does not want to repeat the humiliating experience.

The life lesson here is for parents to encourage their child in all his/her endeavors, but not to overstate the child's actual abilities. This is difficult for the child to overcome, mainly because parents often continue their pattern of overstating the reality of their child's abilities to them in all areas.

I hope this chapter sheds a new light of encouragement to teach these and many other life lessons to your child. My hat is off to all parents in today's world who manage distractions and enjoy both the journey of parenting and marriage.

CHAPTER FIVE
Chess for Developing Logic and Reasoning

Research has found that participating in athletics can have a healthy developmental impact on young children. Sports and athletics promote cooperative play, teamwork, and good sportsmanship while helping to develop brain function and gross motor skills. Sports helps children develop social skills and work cooperatively with others. Group play builds self-esteem, helping your child realize that she's a capable person who is able to accomplish important things. Infancy and childhood are the foundational periods of learning and brain development. Talking, listening, playing, singing, and laughing are all good tools for developing reasoning and logic.

Children differ in the timeline at which they develop, both mentally and physically. Some children may actually start to learn difficult skills like memorization, reasoning, effective communication, and body control at one and a half years and others at six, depending on their developmental timeline and parental influences. Parents are the first teachers for their child and hold the keys that allow children to learn and grow to their potential.

Since 1996, I have championed the teaching of chess, along with sports, to four-year-olds and older as a tool to stimulate brain development. As the director of recreation at The Ritz-Carlton Hotel Company's resort property on Amelia Island, Florida, I implemented the teaching of chess in our Children's Program. The children picked it up quickly, and parents were pleased that their children acquired a skill that involved reason and logic.

During the past three summers, I've taught a tennis camp for The Tennis Key to four- to eight-year-olds at the Westchester Tennis Center in Los Angeles. I specialize in teaching young children chess as a tool for developing reasoning and logic, along with several other games. The children who learn how to play chess truly look forward to playing the game. The children who don't yet know how to play chess are eager to learn because they see their fellow campers having so much fun.

The "why" in teaching chess:
Chess is increasingly being taught in schools because research has proven that it accelerates cognitive function by teaching the skills of logic, multitasking, focus, visualization, hand-eye coordination, and abstract analysis. Consider jump-starting your child's brain development at the age of three and a half to four by introducing the game of chess. Hopefully, the information in this chapter will interest you enough to learn and begin to play chess with your child. In the appendix, I have outlined some basic chess concepts and teaching techniques to get you started.

Parents have often asked me about teaching the game of checkers to their children as a foundation before teaching chess. They are two different games, and, in my opinion, chess offers greater developmental benefits. Most of the parents who asked me this didn't know how to play the game of chess. Of course, there is nothing wrong with teaching checkers first, to hone your teaching skills and gauge your comfort level before tackling chess. But personally, I would teach chess first because children are capable of learning it. Don't discover how to play the game as you teach your child. Teaching is an art, and you need confidence in your skills to translate the ability and confidence to your child. Parents should know the basic rules of how each piece moves and how the board is set up before teaching children how to play the game.

Not only will you learn to play chess, but it will also deepen the relationship between you and your child. You are acting as a playmate first and a parent/teacher second in a nonconfrontational setting. Playing the game of chess stimulates brain development at any age. In sports there is a saying about muscles, "If you don't use it, you'll lose it." Parents, this is even more meaningful with the use or nonuse of the brain!

Begin your chess learning/teaching process with a physical board game. I suggest using an actual chessboard and pieces and not an electronic chess game to start. If using an electronic game, young children aren't exposed to potential motor skill development. The simple act of reaching, picking up a chess piece, and moving it to another square, without knocking over other pieces, is a great learning tool for motor and spatial skills. Many children are visual learners, and as such the actual chess pieces and board show dimensions that are easier to identify and follow. Touch is another sense that will be developed with an actual chess set.

When I experimented with teaching using an electronic chessboard, many younger children became less interested in the game, in part because the electronic device itself was new and somewhat confusing to their young minds. Learning to play chess and learning to use an electronic device can cause stress and actually hinder a child's development. When I introduced chess and electronics, I noticed children were overstimulated.

My mother, a special education teacher at the first to eighth grade level, believed that overstimulation is a learning deterrent. She encouraged parents to limit the number of toys their children played with at one time, to protect them from this sensory overload. She felt that playing with too many toys at the same time affected their ability to focus, to be satisfied with a single toy, and to enjoy creative play. She added that children who have too many toys, clothes, and other material things could suffer as adults by their need to have material things in order to be happy. So, watch for your child not to be overstimulated because that may cause stress instead of fun.

The social benefits of learning chess also will be minimized if learning begins with an electronic device. Verbal communication is especially important to all children at a young age. The number of children in the four- to seven-year-old age range who find it hard to verbalize when asked a question disheartens me. Some children just have a blank stare on their face or shake their head to answer questions. I am concerned that playing against electronic games encourages them to be nonverbal. It is well documented that exposure to too much TV will have a negative effect on overall development. Television is not a good baby-sitter, and the American Academy of Pediatrics recommends no TV exposure before the age of two.

Chess enhances a child's ability to reason and helps your child develop logic awareness both in sports and academics. First, players learn the rules of the movement patterns of their army's pieces. Second, and extremely important, they learn to analyze and evaluate their opponent's moves. This will lead to the development of strategies to overcome their opponent. They are learning how to defeat many obstacles in order to be successful. Chess is a great vehicle for a child to learn the difficult but important skill of multitasking in a single complex task.

Chess exposes children to the mental strategies that athletic champions use to approach sports. If two athletes are equal in athletic ability, and even if one is better than the other, the one who wins is the athlete with the superior mental tools.

Teaching process:
It is extremely important in teaching your child the game to refresh the moves of each of the pieces he/she learned before introducing a new piece. A good way to do this is to ask your child to show you how the pawn moves first. If he/she is correct, give him/her a high five or a sincere comment of "good memory." I like the physical high five over a verbal comment, but both are better than one for most children. Physical contact seems to connect us better with our children. If they don't know the correct pattern in pieces' moves, explain again what the options are.

Frequency of exposure is also important in learning. If you play chess or most other games with your child only once a week, that is not enough review time for him to memorize what he was shown. The names of the pieces and how they move need constant reinforcement for your child to memorize the lessons. A well-structured lesson in which your child has fun learning the basics is the best for learning and retention.

Remember to expose your child to chess in reasonable durations that are fun. In recreation there is a saying, "Do not kill the cat!" Most children like cats and have fun playing with them. But if they play with the cat too long, they will get bored and not want to play with the cat anymore. But if you take the cat away at a point where a child is having a great time, she will be anxious to play with the cat again soon. In other words, stop teaching before your child loses interest.

A good teaching tool is to encourage your children's learning by letting them succeed. Experiencing success also keeps them interested in learning. We all enjoy doing something new, especially if we do it well. As a coach, I have witnessed parents competing with their child and not allow him/her to win. These parents mistakenly believe that their child will be challenged and respond positively. These parents believe that the child beating them is the true sign of accomplishment as a teacher. I call this the "you're not good until you can beat me" attitude. Parents with this attitude usually tell me that their own mother or father wouldn't let them win.

As a parent, it's crucial to make learning fun for your child. If you cannot play and have fun with your child, please do not try to teach him/her. Learning is natural when the experience is engaging and lighthearted. Play is an emotional experience where smiles and laughter are present. Parent disappointment shown to a child when a mistake is made has an indelible impact. Remember, the expression of disappointment doesn't have to be just verbal to devastate a child. It can be a certain look or body language. We speak with more than our words. An unhappy facial expression or a shake of the head can destroy a young child. I find that children are surprisingly astute at recognizing a parent's dissatisfaction. You don't want your child to suffer silently from this painful experience.

If teaching through play is a chore for you, your child will pick up on it and could shut down. If you play with someone and it isn't fun, do you want to play with that person again? And if you have higher expectations than are realistic for your child, the experience of learning will be frustrating for both of you. This is true with anything that you are trying to teach your child.

I can usually tell when parents are good candidates for teaching their children through play. If neither parent appears to be a potentially fun teacher, I will coach the best qualified of the parents. There is a world of difference between adults playing with adults and adults playing with children. Adult play is often about competition. Adult and child play should involve fun and nurturing. I often find that if an adult did not experience fun in play during his own childhood, he may have a hard time playing lightheartedly with his own child.

The quick solution is to have a certified teacher with good references give your child four to ten lessons. During these three- to fifteen-minute lessons only, observe the teacher and how he/she interacts with your child. I suggest that the parent does not get involved during these lessons, unless invited to do so by the teacher. After each lesson, you can debrief with the teacher on how the child reacted to the lesson. I suggest that parents role-play with the teacher by playing the part of the child. This will help both the teacher and the parent evaluate how the parent will react while teaching the child.

Unlike the often slow and intimidating approach to chess, let us learn and teach the rules of movement for each chess piece in individual segments. Then introduce the other pieces one at a time. This will help build the child's memory of all the pieces and their possible moves, so they can play the game with complete armies with confidence.

Another important thing to learning chess is to be able to memorize individual piece movements through efficient reasoning. Being able to articulate that information correctly and quickly is valuable in chess as it is in life situations. Learning chess should be fun, easy to understand, and done at a pace comfortable for each player. After gaining knowledge with practice, the brain is like a muscle that can react more quickly and with greater accuracy.

The key to being able to teach chess to your child is for you to be comfortable with the movements of the pieces and to understand the basics of chess. It is so important for you to practice in advance what you are going to teach your child. You only get one chance to make a first impression. Be prepared to teach and anticipate questions from your children beyond what you plan to teach at each session. And remember, it's OK for not only your child but also you to make mistakes.

Learning through failure is an invaluable tool in sports, games, and especially in our personal lives. In chapter 2, on parenting, remember the Millennials, whose parents basically protected them from failure in almost everything. In the context of teaching your child to play chess, allow your child to succeed, especially with all the quarter-board games and the first five full-board games. Temper your play with your child's improvement from this point forward. I suggest that parents make the games challenging and close. This can be accomplished by not trying to make the game perfect, without mistakes. Start off by allowing your child to capture a few pieces, and then capture some of her pieces. You will be surprised at how quickly your child will learn.

Let us remember how we earlier defined winning for the benefit of your child's development. When we are in the process of learning something mentally or physically and use good effort and good focus, that is winning. Parents and their child should be proud of every improvement made in learning chess and anything else that requires good effort, focus, and improving. Children who believe that good focus and effort on their part translates into improvement develop a great work ethic for a lifetime. Teach your child that it is OK to make mistakes, and that correcting mistakes is part of the learning process!

Interested in getting your child more interested in chess? Talk to the parents of your child's friends and offer to teach their child along with yours. The powers of peer pressure and playing with friends are awesome ingredients for motivation to play and learn most everything.

For the beginner, the best tactic is remembering how each piece moves and learning from mistakes. Trying not to repeat the same mistakes over and over again is important. In teaching your child to play chess, winning is not as important as learning how the pieces move and improving one's understanding of the game. Winning is a result of proper practice, good effort, focus, and improving one's strategy. Make chess a part of your family life today.

These are some well-documented benefits of young children learning how to play chess:

- It improves the development of the brain

- It helps to build memory skills

- It develops higher concentration levels

- It aids in developmental and critical thinking

- It promotes problem solving in many different areas

- It strengthens the ability of analysis and evaluation

- It encourages patience and discipline

- It helps children identify patterns of behavior

- It develops and enhances players' IQ levels

- It adds to a child's emotional intelligence level

- It helps underachievers gain self-confidence

- It challenges gifted children to expand their abilities

- It is especially valuable for adults as we age and helps reverse memory loss

- It helps in the competitive adult working world by reducing stress

- It helps children with ADHD improve focus and hone their creative drive

Chess is a great educational tool year-round. A great time for parents to introduce and focus on chess with their children is during the summer. It is traditionally an educational break for children. However, most parents and educators agree that the structure of learning should not be paused or halted during the summer. Other year-round brain builders are: reading to your child, singing, music, storytelling, and creative writing. Repetition is the key in the continual development of brain function and motor skills.

CHAPTER SIX
Parent Teaching – Stage One

Birth to Four Years Old

In this chapter I offer a chronological list of parent-led activities for a child starting at three months old. The purpose of the activities is to promote physical, athletic, and cognitive development for a lifetime.

The activities range from lengths of one and a half minutes to ten minutes, depending on your child's age, abilities, and activity level. Frequency in terms of the number of days per week or times per day will vary with each child's developmental stage. An important success factor in this process is the parent's patience, persistence, and ability to have fun while conducting each activity.

The best way to use the information in this and the next two chapters is to start with this chapter. Work with your child in every activity or game to gradually accomplish each developmental goal. The reason for starting at the beginning of this chapter, even though your child may be five years old, is that many activities require mastering a prerequisite activity, before a more complex movement can be effectively mastered.

Often, a skipped skill, like a lack of good balance, will hinder all walking/running, change of direction, and stopping abilities. Another example of a skipped skill that will definitely affect your child's ability to learn in many areas is a child not knowing his left hand and foot from his right hand and foot. A solid foundation is the most important factor in building athletic skills and in anything we learn.

I can assure you that the thrill of having a child will be rekindled every time you see him/her improve. I say this with 100 percent certainty because I felt this with my own children. Whether I was teaching my daughters how to swim or new social skills, I felt a joy and pride in my girls. Later, as part of the driver's training, aside from driving skills, I taught them how to change a flat tire and the basics of auto mechanics. The training helped my daughters become more skilled drivers and made me feel that they were safer on the road. Even today, when their car needs repairs and they understand what the mechanics are talking about, their understanding helps them avoid being overcharged. To this day, I still get an emotional high from seeing the improvement of my students. It is fun to help a child, a teen, or an adult build emotional confidence and athleticism.

So now that we are on the same page, let us review the terminology specific to this and the next two chapters.

Brain: The brain is the center of our nervous system and holds the key to our accomplishment potential in life. The processes that the brain is involved in include memory, language, problem solving, breathing, heart function, and our body's movement. The health and fitness industry touts the slogan "use it or lose it," which is so apropos for the strength, effectiveness, and resilience of our brain. Play also trains us to cope with the unpredictable, thus making the brain more behaviorally flexible and increasing learning capacity. Brain activity and exercise are especially important at the beginning and during the latter parts of our lives.

Cognition: The development of mental processes that include memory, attention, the ability to communicate in multiple languages, problem solving, and the analysis of factors for the best solutions.

Athleticism: Involves complex coordination, spatial skills, balance, movement, flexibility, activeness, suppleness, strength, aerobic capacity, and body control.

Motor skills: Fine and gross motor skills are a learned sequence of movements that, when combined, help one perform a specific task. Fine motor skills involve the use of the small muscle groups to brush one's teeth or tie shoestrings. Gross motor skills refer to the large muscle groups used to balance, walk, or ride a bike.

Motor skill learning stages:

- Cognitive stage: The primary stage where thoughts start the process with the question, "What do I want to do?" Considerable cognitive activity is required, especially for a young child, so that she can determine appropriate ways to accomplish a specific task. The optimal ways are retained and inefficient ways are often discarded. The performance improves in a short amount of time with proper repetition.

- Associative stage: In this stage, a person has determined the most effective way to do the task and starts to make subtle adjustments in performance. Improvements are more gradual and movement becomes more consistent in time with continual proper practice.

- Automatic stage: This is where tasks are being performed with little or no thought and executed efficiently. Reaching this phase may take several months or years, depending on the task and the quality of repetitions. It is possible that this stage may never be reached in many movement sequences. A child's abilities, mechanics, or coaching may not always be up to the task desired. Examples of this stage include walking, talking, playing a recreational sport, or sending a text message.

- Eye-hand coordination: This involves the coordinated vision and hand movement to execute a task. Babies start their quest in this coordination category when they reach for their bottle and items in their crib.

- Eye-foot coordination: Same principles as in eye-hand coordination and includes sports and everyday abilities such as walking, running, changing direction, and going up or down steps.

- Body balance: I believe this is the most important quality to have for athletic success. Only with exceptional balance can an athlete reach her potential. What some people consider being a "natural athlete" is simply a child or person with better-than-average body balance at an early age. This high degree of balance allows separate parts of the body to move independently while remaining completely balanced.

- Core strength: The muscles involved in core strength are the abdominals, the hip complex, and the lower back. Core strength is important from the infant stage of our lives through our entire life. The lack of appropriate core strength affects balance, head control, and posture. Poor posture can contribute greatly to back pain. The core muscles transfer the movement from the lower body to the upper body. The kinetic chain or the human movement system is dependent on the strength of the core muscles. Ironically, the core strength muscle group is the weakest in the body, even in today's generation of professional athletes.

- Spatial skills: The ability to visually pinpoint an object, either moving or still, in our environment and connect our hands, feet, or other body parts to it. It also allows us to avoid objects coming toward us.

- Quickness of motion: Muscle fibers are defined as fast-twitch or slow-twitch. Fast-twitch are credited for an ability to sprint fast and slow-twitch are recognized as a key to a distance runner's success. Regardless of the distribution of muscle fibers, anybody can improve his/her quickness through practice of anticipation and a combination of visual and hearing acuity. Often, young children with that "deer in the headlights" look on their face are not in the moment and are not expecting anything to happen. With some parental coaching, this can change in a very short time.

- Complex coordination: These skills are manipulative skills such as throwing, kicking, catching, dribbling, jumping rope, and tumbling.

- Body management: These skills, such as flexibility, balance, stretching, and strength development and retention, are important skills that need to be practiced for one's entire life.

Hopefully, these terms will help you connect the dots in creating a development plan for your child, as well as help you focus on areas that will aid your child in maintaining positive exercise habits and athleticism for a lifetime.

From a chronological standpoint, your child's mental and athletic ability is triggered at birth. After birth, the brain is engaged with the gross motor skills of simply moving the head and sucking on a mother's or a bottle's nipple. This sucking for milk affords a child nutrition and security. This explains why a pacifier is difficult to take away from a child, since the child associates the sucking with comfort and security. A child's brain is engaged in cognitive memory and analysis, and learning is in full bloom.

From birth onward, your baby's brain is being shaped. A baby's brain consists of a hundred billion brain cells called neurons. These neurons interconnect with one another, like roads and bridges. The more connections the neurons make, the smarter your child becomes. The formation of these connections is triggered when your baby is exposed to an environment that is rich with colors, sounds, smells, movement, and touch. The simple acts of talking to your baby, rocking her to sleep, singing her a song, and touching her fingers actually build your baby's brain. Introducing your baby to a rich environment filled with multisensory experience is called infant stimulation.

You can begin stimulating your infant's brain development at as early as three months old by teaching her how to use sign language. This is a great tool that I was not aware of half a century ago during my children's early years. Some good hand signals to start with are the ones that help your child get her basic needs met with simple hand gestures: milk and eat, followed by Mom and Dad. Introduce the signs for book and music, especially when you start reading with your child. Touching a child's mouth, nose, ear, or chin and saying those facial parts will lead to brain stimulation and early communication skills. A child's ability to display those signs varies by individual abilities and a parent's repetition.

Let me address the myth that babies are ignorant, cute blobs that are aware of very little. Babies are much the opposite, according to articles published in the scientific magazine Nature by Karen Wynn, director of Yale University's Infant Cognitive Center. In 1992, her studies of babies at five months showed that they could do simple addition with small sets of physical objects.

Wynn's research showed that 75 percent of the babies tested have a preference for good behavior over bad behavior. This groundbreaking study was featured on CBS's 60 Minutes on November 18, 2012. I cite this research for two reasons: first, to support my encouragement that you do not underestimate your baby's ability to learn; second, to provide a basis for recommending that you remember that your baby is watching, listening, and learning much sooner than you think. Parents should be aware that babies are processing every word they hear around them.

I would like to offer a word of caution about overloading your child with too many experiences in a short period of time. The brain is like a muscle group, that overloading a group of muscles will cause them to fail. The brain should be developed slowly to ensure proper development and for maximum proficiency. Each part of the brain should be used to develop the entire brain, as you would develop the muscles in a baby's body.

In this comparison of the brain to muscles, even seldom-used muscles must be developed so they can be used when needed. There are periods of neurological opportunity that enhance the brain's plasticity and aptitude for a lifetime. The period between three months and six years is a very fertile period. But do not overload their experience.

Overloading your children with too many new concepts in their early developmental months and years is a deterrent to their learning. Too many new concepts introduced at the same time will tend to confuse young children. In fact, they may have a tendency to shut down if they are not given time to process the incoming information. Each child has her own way of learning and understanding that will be short-circuited if the flow of information is too rapid.

The extreme opposite would be underloading your child. We know the results of underfeeding a child. Undernourishment will affect the development of the body and all its systems. The same is true with their learning process. Children need to be fed information in palatable and regulated amounts in order to both understand and retain that information.

Physical milestones will dominate your child's development over the first nine months as he learns to move and control his head, which leads to rolling over and sitting. Spatial skills start in the first few months, especially when a child is being fed. Self-feeding will increase your child's spatial skills and complex coordination.

When your child can sit on the floor with legs apart, roll a ball toward her to start honing her spatial skills with an object in motion. Later, teach her to roll the ball back to you.

When your child has good neck and core strength, hold her trunk and move her through the air like she is flying. An advanced version of this exercise includes having her make wings with her arms, and flapping them. Another adaptation is to have her kick her legs in a flutter kick to simulate swimming.

Standing and walking without your help may occur around the ninth month. By fifteen months, your child should be able to throw a ball underhanded and track incoming objects like a ball or beanbag.

Your role as a dual-goal coach starts when she can sit balanced for four minutes and walk with moderate balance.

Between eighteen and twenty-four months, your child can walk up and down steps, run with more coordination, jump off a bottom step, move side to side, and experience the "terrible twos" by possibly throwing tantrums. This is a good time to start teaching the right, left, and perhaps the middle of their bodies.

Gross motor skills and brain development during the first few months to two years can be enhanced by the following fun activities, but only in time periods of short duration.

Basic list:

- Mirroring parent in: clapping hands, clapping feet, touching nose, ears, and mouth, and pointing to eyes, feet, elbows, hands, etc.

- Bubble burst (played in a bubble bath): catching the floating bubbles and/or rubber ducky in the tub

- Flying, with parent securely holding child with both hands while moving through the air

- Sitting ball stop and roll or toss back

- Finger and toe math games like One Little, Two Little Indians

- Beanbag tosses to child

- Safe pillow fights, with the child winning most of the battles

- Play dough (supervised to ensure the play dough is not eaten), and numbered and lettered blocks

- Walk, jump, run, skip, and moving side to side

- Games that reinforces complex movement and knowledge of the left and right sides of the body

Beginning at three years old, a child can increase his/her coordination proficiency by going down stairs reciprocally, riding a bike with training wheels, catching and throwing a ball, jumping with two feet, and balancing briefly on one foot. Playing tag is a good developmental game to increase the ability to change directions, stop, and start. With added repetitions, complicated movements will become more consistent. Remember that a parent's focus at this stage is to improve their child's basic motor skills and fitness by implementing exercises and games that are fun.

A fundamental movement and spatial skill activity to do with your child is as follows. With her facing you and her legs spread out past her shoulders, roll a ball between her legs. The object of this activity is to have her move sideways in order to keep the rolling ball between her feet without the ball touching either foot. Do this several times, then roll the ball so she has to move quickly in order for the ball to go between her legs. This activity is a prerequisite for the next game.

A fun game to play with your child and at least one other child is Caterpillar. The game is played with a minimum of six to ten tennis balls. Your child should be facing you with his feet a little more than shoulder distance apart and his playmate one to two feet behind him, with his feet apart. Your child is the head of the caterpillar and the other is the tail. The challenge for them is to shuffle sideways into position so that the tossed ball rolls between their legs. If the ball hits the foot of one of them, that child is then the tail of the caterpillar. This game guarantees smiling faces! I use it a lot, especially in summer tennis camps.

Activities to increase proficiency are:

- Playing hopscotch.

- Walking forward, backward, and from side to side both on tiptoes, heels, and regular steps.

- Kicking and stopping a ball with either foot.

- Running both five-yard sprints and ten-yard slow runs.

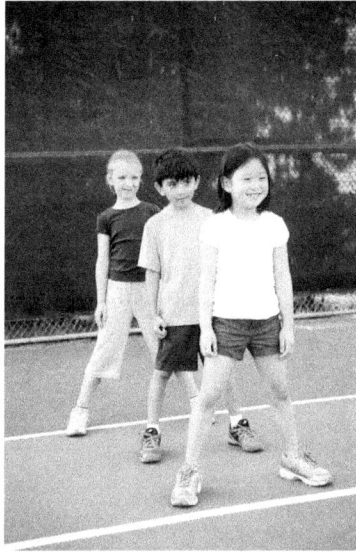

Ready to Play Caterpillar

- Walking the path of a W-shaped obstacle course with the parent facing the pattern. A young child will see it as an M-shaped pattern. Use five cones as shown in the picture below. With the parent looking at the W, start her on the outside of the top left cone of the W and have her walk to the outside or left of the first bottom cone in the W. Have her take a side step below the cone and go backward to the left side of the middle top cone. She then goes behind the top middle cone, sidesteps to the left, and walks forward to the left side of the second bottom cone. She goes below that cone, sidesteps to the left, and goes backward to the outside right side of the top cone on the far right side of the W. Repeat this pattern several times until she can navigate it easily, then reverse the pattern until she can navigate it with ease. When your child masters the pictured footwork pattern, introduce her to moving quickly through the cones. Time each of her efforts moving through the W to the left. Then time her moving to the right of the W in order to track her improvement in both directions.

Cones in W Pattern

- Riding a bike and walking on the beach or in a park with parent.

- Storytelling. This is a good activity that you and your child can act out, preferably with music. In the story, introduce a new person or animal and both of you imitate the new character by making noises and movement of the character. This is great for his/her imagination and your creativity.

- Playing wheelbarrow, with you holding your child's ankles and your child walking forward on his hands.

- Only direct speech from a human will enhance the language centers of the brain, not TVs, CDs or DVDs. Use the TV only when you need a break.

- Any reflex game, such as stopping a rolling ball with either foot and/or hand before it stops rolling.

- Don't forget the game called Etch A Sketch. It's great for developing motor skills, spatial skills, and creativity.

We hear the term natural athlete used often to describe a young child who has coordination skills several levels above his/her peers. Yes, there is a genetic disposition that may contribute to this temporary state. I say "temporary" because, if properly trained, all children have the potential to do well athletically and in sports. The child who may be labeled a "natural athlete" very possibly has had the advantage of early physical development designed by his/her parents, or by circumstance has an older sibling who played with him/her. In either case, complex coordination and spatial skills can be taught.

I have found that children who have advanced skills and excel in sports at a young age may have trouble maintaining that success in sports in high school, and college. I believe this occurs because both the parent and the child believe that he/she has a special talent. By definition, natural athletes will find that sports come easily to them. This becomes a stumbling block the older they get. Why? Often, they lack the needed work ethic to continue to improve. They had been good without even trying. Meanwhile, children who didn't have as natural an ability, and who had been working hard to improve, develop exceptional work habits. These children often surpass the natural athletes in college and in the pros.

The result of your dual-goal parenting now kicks into full gear with your four-year-old. In the cognitive and physical areas, you'll probably be able to see a big difference between your child and other children in the same age group. Remember that your child's effort and focus are equally as important as both you and your child having fun together.

CHAPTER SEVEN
Parent Teaching – Stage Two

———

Starting Around Four Years Old

By being your child's dual-goal coach during her baby and childhood years, you will have accomplished several meaningful goals. You will have helped give your child the priceless gifts of accelerated brain development, communication skills, and physical development. You also will have set the stage for developing a deeper bond with your child. In my life experiences, the most cherished lessons you can teach are by example. Your child will learn to set goals and develop an understanding that applying them every day will serve her for the rest of her life.

Allow me to demystify the process of becoming a successful dual-goal coach for your child's cognitive and athletic development. Foremost is identifying opportunities to teach life lessons and enhancing your ability to play like a child with your child. Avoid expecting too much from her, and especially showing your disappointment. She will absorb not only what you plan to teach, but also will observe your demeanor, the words you use, and tone and inflection in your voice. Your joy and disappointment also will be a part of what she is learning. Remember, in the previous chapter, the fact that a baby as young as three months can detect helpful and unhelpful behavior. You may want to stop using baby talk for communication with your child, if you do use it. Many parents find that it is a difficult habit to correct.

The duration of the game or activity and the enthusiasm, or lack thereof, that you exhibit, will create the game environment. Recognize when to stop playing a game with your child based on her attention span. And let us not forget the positive feedback for good effort when deserved. A dual-goal coach is the equivalent of being your child's parent, life coach, and CEO. It would be a big missed opportunity for both parent and child not to take advantage of being a dual-goal coach for her. You can't expect your child's school and other venues to be responsible for her development.

Let me be quite candid here: the purpose of this chapter is to assist your child to be athletic and to establish exercise as a lifetime habit. It is not to groom your child to be a professional athlete and support you for the rest of your life. The key lesson of being physically active, which can be taught in this stage and will serve your child for the rest of her life, is that she can get satisfaction playing sports without even wanting to be the best. Show her that focus and effort in practice and in playing are their own rewards.

Almost any activity is good for her, but proper mechanics are extremely important, even at this level. Poor mechanics will catch up to anyone in the form of injury or in the lack of development and improvement. This is one of two concerns that I have with an uncertified athletic trainer teaching others. The second concern is that the instructor has a fun personality and easily engages with children.

With young children there are missed opportunities for them to learn to be responsible for their own self-care. This is caused at times by the theory that it is easier and quicker to do certain things for them. Examples are: feeding him, tying his shoestrings, dressing him, and brushing his teeth. Learning the fine motor skills takes more time for the child and patience in teaching for the parents.

Developmental Games
Since most body functions start with the engaging of the brain, I strongly suggest exposing your four-year-old to chess. The appendix contains a guide to a process to teach your child this wonderful developmental game. The emphasis at this age is the concept of the movement of one chess piece at a time in the correct pattern and the eye-hand coordination skills needed to move the pieces. While playing, challenge him by asking him to use his non-dominant hand often.

Other brain development activities include playing checkers, cards, and board games such as Monopoly (the classic edition) and the children's edition of Scrabble. Artwork of any type, music, and reading are often underused developmental tools for boys.

I like teaching numbers by using tennis balls. With a marker, put a large number on a ball in several places. Have him sit on the floor with his legs apart. Roll the ball slowly toward him so he can see the number. Ask him to call out the number on the ball as soon as he recognizes it. You can add excitement and science by having your child track a rolling ball with a flashlight in a dim or dark room. These processes will improved his visual tracking and focus, and assist in the learning of numbers.

The basic concepts of addition and subtraction also can be implemented with the use of a small group of balls. Adding or subtracting balls in a group will help with visual learning. You can teach your child the alphabet the same way. Numbered and lettered blocks are also great tools for learning both what is imprinted on them and the motor skills associated with stacking them. Blocks and an erector set were my favorite toys as a child. Legos weren't available yet in the 1940s.

Games played while traveling in a vehicle can be used to learn words, shapes, colors, and numbers, and to develop recognition skills. Your child will learn to identify many types of objects and will develop memory. If there is traffic and you, as the driver, need to focus solely on driving, choose a different passenger to play with your child. Play the game first while on a walk with your child so she feels comfortable and wants to play it. Ask questions like: "What color is that sign?" "What words are on the sign?" "How many cars or trucks are on the right side of our car?" "What state is the license plate of the car in front of us from?" "Do you see a fence or an animal around us?" For a memory check, ask your child the color of the first or second sign that she saw.

It is worth mentioning again that for each activity or game to be fun for your child, it has to be fun for you. Have age-appropriate expectations for your child's ability to learn. Be a dual-goal teacher by teaching communication skills as part of the game. Have a plan and be well versed in each activity. Be aware of when to start, review, and stop an activity. Be flexible with both your start and stop times.

Specifically, make sure that your child is fed, rested, and not distracted before starting. It is no time to try to multitask. As far as the time to stop, do not be governed by what you want to accomplish. Be aware of your child's attention span, which will vary, and stop while he is still having fun. If you wait until he is distracted or bored, you take the chance of your child not wanting to play that game again.

In working with your child's ability to be in controlled motion, change directions, or stop, you have probably found that balance is the most important factor. By balance, I mean complex-coordination movement in a rhythmic, effortless, and controlled manner. You have started your child's journey to learn balance while coaching her to walk as a baby. It is time now, if you have not started already, to expand on her movement experiences. Balance involves four different body systems: vision, the vestibular system, proprioceptors, and core muscles.

- Vision allows us to be aware of our environment and what is in motion and not in motion. During everyday activities such as eating, driving, and walking, we judge distance and depth perception.

- The vestibular system refers to the inner ear. These canals are filled with a fluid that moves when our head moves. The fluid triggers little hairs in the ear canal that send signals to the eye muscles. This allows the eye to focus on objects as our head moves. This process allows for good eye-hand coordination and tracking skills.

- Proprioceptors are sensors in our joints and tendons that communicate our movement to our brain and muscles.

- Core muscles are comprised of the abdominal, mid, and lower back muscles. Marginally, the hips, shoulder, and neck muscles come into play. Core muscles' endurance and strength or the lack thereof greatly affect body balance.

Parent-Taught Games and Activities

Since children enjoy games I would like to suggest a balance game that has many names. For four-year-old girls, I call the game Ballerina, and for boys I call it The Karate Kid. For a child six or older, I use the name Balancing Challenge. Since you are facilitating the game, call it whatever you feel relates to his world. With your child standing with his feet shoulder distance apart and his arms by his side, ask him to lift his right leg so his knee is even with his belly button, then return his right leg to the floor. At this point, demonstrate what you asked him to do. Then ask him to repeat what you asked him to do, to help him understand the game and to improve memory and communication skills. It also reinforces his knowing his right side of the body from his left.

High Knee Balance

His ability to balance will last for only a few seconds. To engage his memory, ask him which leg he is balancing on several times, to reinforce that information. At this stage, no matter how well or poorly he does, tell him "nice try." Now, demonstrate doing the same thing, but move your arms to help you stay balanced. Ask him to try to balance lifting his leg and using his arms to stay balanced. Again, use "nice try" for his positive feedback and self-esteem.

As a dual-goal coach you have the perfect opportunity to teach the time components of seconds, minutes, and hours. In playing my games with a time factor, learning seconds will be especially helpful and educational.

I suggest actually timing his first try and subsequent tries to establish a baseline time. Show him how to use his arms to balance and how his times will increase. Tracking his times will show him the improvement that he made. It also will help him to understand the measurement of time. After no more than one to one and a half minutes of attempts on his right leg, have him balance on his left leg with the same teaching process. Do not exceed a total of four minutes at first with this game. A child learns when something is fun, not drudgery. One more way to keep it fun is to record the results of the session by writing them down or videoing the highlights of the session. Some parents take a picture of their child doing the games and post them in his/her room or on the refrigerator. This helps strengthen the child and parent bonding process. It's also the first step in teaching your child how to track and set goals. And yes, goal setting can begin at four years old.

How frequently you play games with your child will vary with your schedule and how much you and your child enjoy the game days. It may be a minimum of four days a week and up to seven days a week. Hopefully, your child will look forward to her game days, as the routine becomes a positive habit and a family ritual. I like calling these developmental times game days so that when she plays a competitive sport in the future, she associates game days with fun and not feelings of pressure or competition.

Another beginning game for learning balance is a game that I call Grand Canyon. Stimulate your child's imagination by having her pretend that she is one hundred feet in the air, walking on a tiny rope above the canyon. The game can be more fun and educational if you embellish a story about the Grand Canyon. The game is her walking, preferably barefoot and toe-to-heel, for a distance of three to six feet. It's a fun way to improve her balance skills. For a variation of the exercise, have your child walk heel-to-toe. Simply walking up and down steps encourages good balance. Until now, most of your child's walking has been forward, with some deviation to the left or right of a straight line.

The Grand Canyon game is used until your child masters it and it becomes easy. If it is too easy, it will become boring for your child. To add challenge to the game, have her cover one eye with her hand. I suggest that you try the game yourself to help gauge the difficulty experienced by your young child. Other games that I suggest are used at the professional level in sports. Your ultimate goal should be to create a number of games your child enjoys that encourage physical development of her upper body, core muscles, lower body, and aerobic capacity.

The Line game incorporates forward and backward movement, the split step, and teaches the awareness of the left foot and right foot. A small space of three feet will accommodate this game. Make two lines three feet apart. Your child will start on the back line, go to the front line, and stop with what you call out. You may call his left foot, right foot, or a split step. A split step is basically a hop that temporarily stops motion and allows movement to be restarted quickly. He will always return to the line where he started. Your child will learn the basics of demonstrating his knowledge of what foot to use. Speed up the rhythm as your child's confidence increases. In fact, a fun factor while your child is on the front line with his right foot is to change the original foot that you called out by saying, "I meant the left foot (or split step)." The brain is challenged to send the correct message to the nerves and muscles.

Make sure that the way in which you invite your child to play the game is appealing and convincing. Instead of saying, "Do you want to play?" which makes it easy to say no, consider saying, "Let's play." When there is a choice of several games, I suggest framing your question this way. "Do you want to play (game name) or (other game name)"? This is particularly important to do as your child gets older.

Now embellish your child's skills by introducing backward movement with the Forward and Backward game. With nine to fifteen feet of movement area, create a straight horizontal line on the floor, grass, sand, or concrete. Establish A as the point at the start of the horizontal line, B as the middle point on the line, and C as the end of the line to the right. Demonstrate starting on B, walking to C, and stopping. Then walk backward to B, leaning forward while going backward. A good cue for leaning forward is to tell your child to stick her butt out while going backward only. Then walk backward from position B to A. Last, go forward from A to B.

A   B   C
_____

Layout for Line Games

Now let her do B to C and back to B, then B to A and back to B. You will be teaching the alphabet and new words, as well as forward and backward movement. Later, you can substitute other letters of the alphabet or numbers in the three positions. When your child masters this exercise, to stimulate her brain and memory include starting her movement with her right or left foot.

Timing the exercise will heighten your child's interest and allow you to track her improvement. Consider keeping a record book of her times and games. It's like keeping a photo album for family memories.

The next progression is to introduce a split step as a way of stopping on all the positions. The split step is used in many sports as an advanced movement.

After your child can hop with relatively good balance, introduce hopping sideways and forward. Using the five-foot line on the ground, have your child start the Line Hopping game on either side of the line in position A. Demonstrate the game by hopping forward from one side of the line to the other. Continue this until you have reached the other end of the line. Ask your child to do what you did. She will find that hopping sideways is a little more difficult than hopping directly forward. You want to keep your child challenged. The next subtle progression is to have her do the Backward game, which is the reverse of the Line Hopping game.

Naming the games will help you remember their format. Most importantly, your child will remember the games by name, especially the ones she likes. This will prove to be very helpful to you. The games she does not mention may be the ones that she feels are too difficult. These games should be done after a game that your child really enjoys. You can also rename a game that she doesn't like in order for her not to be anxious about it. Now you have enough games to begin your child's circuit training. Just alternate each game that your child learns into one multifaceted circuit or routine.

The next progression that I suggest is Stop and Go. This game focuses on her running both forward and backward in a straight line with stops at A, B or C. Watch for the use of good technique. Encourage your child to lean forward with her head and shoulders while going backward and then doing a balanced split step. Running both forward and backward should be done on the balls of her feet. I find that a lot of athletic children run flat-footed because they have not been taught how to run properly. This activity will increase their quickness, speed, agility, and balance.

Increasing the distances in Stop and Go from A to B and to C will be required as your child becomes more proficient with the game. The duration at this level might be three to four minutes for the four- and five-year-olds. Remember to quit when they are having fun. If you end a game when your child is tired or not having fun, she will remember that and may not want to do it again. This advice is the same for all games and activities in this age range.

Be creative and use variations with all games. In the aforementioned games, add picking up a small ball at position B and placing it at position C to increase the fun and range of motion. Have your child pick up and put down an object with different hands for the benefit of complex coordination and learning her left from her right side of her body. Another skill to practice is to have your child hop on one foot to point A, B, and C, instead of walking or running. Do not forget the split step in this game. Tossing a tennis ball to your child while she does the exercise will add difficulty and develop her spatial and tracking skills. It also increases the fun factor if your child can touch or preferably catch the ball.

This leads me to an important teaching skill. If you structure a game and your child fails miserably, change the game to reduce the difficulty. Do not continue to let your child fail at this age level. After she can do the less difficult version of the game, reintroduce the more difficult version in gradual stages. My dad was particularly good at this method of teaching. In today's world, this teaching method is referred to as scalability, when we teach a group of students and each student is at a different level. All my games are designed to be fun and elevate a child's ability to play the game and improve self-confidence.

Proper running form is the most overlooked area in the development of coordination, flexibility, fitness, and strength in 99 percent of the thousands of children I watch. Running is one of the three basic physical development skills, along with throwing and jumping. This poor form can be attributed to the loss of children's playtime outdoors and a lot less supervised physical activity in schools and after-school programs. Lifestyle changes have created and allowed the addiction to media-centered child care. Children today are less physically active because they are playing video games, watching TV, and using computers rather than playing outside with their friends. The distraction of nonphysical active play is eroding our youth's health and fitness.

I watch coaches in every sport where running is involved and very few of them teach children how to run properly. Children frequently run with the same leg and foot stride used as though they were walking rapidly. This heel striking will cause a stride that literally puts the brakes on forward motion. As a remedy, I find that running barefoot gives runners a natural and correct stride. It will allow the runner to feel the correct way to run. Improving coordination also will allow better foot placement on the ground.

Running with little or incorrect arm motion is a common mistake. The arms should be kept close to the body and should move forward and backward from the shoulders, not from the elbow joint. Shoulders should be relaxed, especially while sprinting. The wrists and hands should be relaxed. Having good arm movement will affect a runner's speed and balance.

Correct Form; Incorrect Form

Weak core muscles can cause leaning forward too much. The ability to run properly is not only important to play most any sport, but for safety and a child's self-esteem. Safety comes into play when a car or another object appears out of nowhere and is coming directly toward a child. Moving quickly can spare a child bodily injury and even save a child's life. All too often I see children not playing fun games with their friends either because they can't run or are embarrassed about their physical skills and choose not to participate. It's important to work with your child and help her learn the correct way to run. And by all means, if you are unsure of how to coach, ask a certified trainer to assist.

The Shuffle Game is the next basic balance game, to teach lateral movement with the shuffle or side step. The shuffle is done by stepping out the outside foot, then bringing the inside foot in the same direction. Continue this pattern until the destination is reached. Then go in the opposite direction. Make sure that the feet do not touch, because this may cause stumbling. I suggest using the same configuration of a straight line, with A, B, and C moving laterally along the line. Make sure that your child's hips are in line with the direction she is going. Use the same verbal keys as before to start and stop her.

After your child does the exercise with little or no trouble, add a quart beverage container with water or sand in it to act as a hurdle. This will increase the difficultly of the exercise. The water or sand will simply help the bottle stay on the line when kicked. Place one container mid-way between the A and B positions. Now ask her to do the exercise. After a few successful tries, add another container between the A and C positions. The containers will encourage her to lift her feet higher to go over them.

Side Lunge: Stand with your feet together, then move your right foot straight out to the side, keeping your left leg straight and both feet flat on the ground. Lower your backside until it is level with your right knee and your chest, shoulders, and head are up. Push up with your right leg and go back to the starting position. Now reverse the starting leg to go in the opposite direction. Repeat four to six times.

Inchworm: With your feet shoulder distance apart, bend forward and put both hands on the ground. Keeping your arms and legs straight, walk forward with your hands until you are in a push-up position and stop. Then walk your hands back toward your feet until they touch or come close to each other. Repeat three to five times.

A good coordination and brain builder is the Colored Ball Game. This game involves three balls, each a different color.

- The red ball indicates catch it with the right hand.

- The green ball indicates catch it with the left hand.

- The blue ball indicates catch it with both hands.

With your child standing four to six feet opposite you, show her the red ball, hesitate, then toss it to her right side. Do the same with each of the other balls. As your child gets better at reacting and catching, speed up tossing the balls.

Perhaps the one game most enjoyed by the four- to ten-year-old age groups that I coach is a game I call I'm Awesome. It encourages the development of memory, self-esteem, spatial skills, lateral movement, eye-hand coordination, and focus. It has aerobic benefits and most importantly, pure fun! To play, a space ranging from ten to eighteen feet wide and six to ten feet deep is needed, with a wall, garage door, or fence as a backstop. You also will need six to ten tennis balls. Inside a garage or in front of a garage door is a perfect spot. Your child should be standing in the middle of the width of the space and to the back of it.

I'm Awesome is a game all children seem to enjoy. The game is best played with two or more, even with older children or adults. A perfect number of players is three to four, which avoids the boredom of not being continuously active. To motivate your child to play physical games, invite one of her friends or neighbors to play the game with him/her.

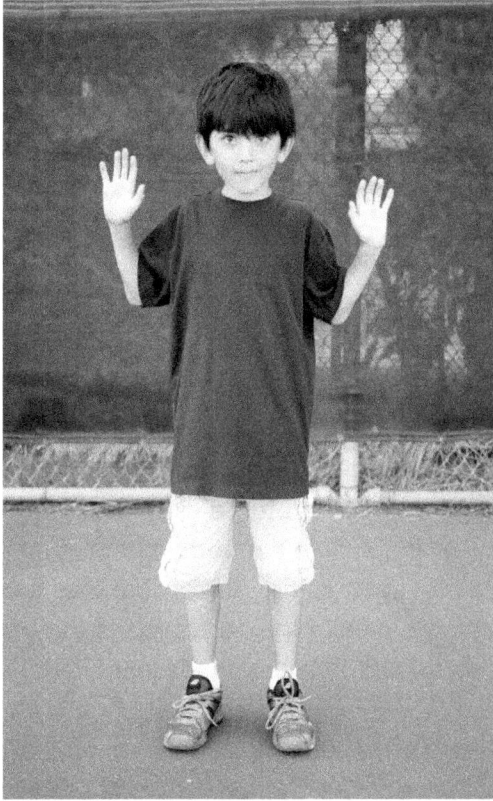

Ready to Play

The rules of the game are simple. Four balls will be tossed, alternating to the right side of your child's body, then to his left side. The balls should be tossed close to him so he can touch them. As he improves, toss the balls farther away from him. His natural tendency will be to swing at the balls; this takes a little more skill, so give her a high five when he connects. Explain before the game is played that if he touches all four balls with the correct hand that will count as a total of four touches. After all four balls are tossed, ask him, "What are you?" His response is based on how many balls she touched.

- Touching all four balls makes his response "super awesome."

- Touching three out of the four balls makes his response "awesome."

- Touching two balls out of the four makes his response "great."

- Touching one ball, or missing all four balls, his response is, "I will do better next time."

This process of being responsible to improve his mistakes is an invaluable life lesson and can be fun.

While showing him four balls, have him repeat after you, his response when all four are touched, then three, then two, and when one or no balls are touched. This will help him remember his responses and help build his math skills of subtraction. Adjust your toss based on his ability to move and touch the ball. In the beginning of the game, always toss the balls so he can touch them with moderate effort.

The last level of the game is adding a bonus round that requires that the first four balls be touched. The degree of difficulty should be dramatically increased for each ball tossed after the fourth ball. Any number after the fourth ball changes your child's response to "superduper awesome." After eight balls, it's "superduperduper awesome." To add difficulty to the game, fake a toss in one direction and toss the ball in the opposite direction. Some children can touch up to sixteen balls. One caution when facilitating this game: watch to make sure your child does not stumble over balls on the ground.

For advanced movement, combine the Shuffle game and the Line game to make the Compass game. This will initially be very challenging for your child, so be patient. Combining the games gives a platform to learn the Compass game and the directions of north, south, east, and west.

Add a vertical line across the middle of the horizontal line, giving you a perfect four-directional compass to move on. Start her where the north and south line intersects the east and west line. Ask her to move in the desired direction, and then back to where she started.

Depending on her language skills a four- or five-year-old can get this game after a few tries. And remember that it is OK for her to make mistakes. Later, try teaching compass directions and the degrees in angles, to help accelerate mathematic learning. This format also can be used to introduce the concept of telling time and showing where the small hand and large hand are on a clock or watch. Remember, your child is a sponge and can learn just about anything if presented properly.

Another one of my favorite games for four-year-olds and above is called Look, Mom (or Dad), No Hands. This game is your child getting up off the floor without the use of his hands. This is a great game for balance, when he is able to do it. Try it yourself and see how difficult it can be to get up with no hands. Doing it yourself will help you gauge your child's ability based on other activities he does with you. This game has no shelf life and can be used to keep one physically fit.

The game of jacks is a great tool to teach eye-hand coordination. My only caution is that your child must have outgrown the stage of putting objects in his mouth. Have him play the game with either hand after he gains a comfortable ability with his dominant hand.

For lower body balance, play an outdoor kicking game called Goalie. All that is needed is a medium-size ball and a cardboard box. Create a goal by turning a box on its side, with a closed back and open front so a ball can roll into it. Have your child stand three feet away from the box and gently kick the ball into it. Record how many time the ball goes in the box out of three tries. Teach how to control the kick and the math aspect of the number of times in the box out of the number of tries. When he does three in out of three tries, move the box backward a foot to increase the distance of the kick. Have him try with his right foot and then his left foot. When he becomes proficient in kicking, an option is to use a smaller box as a target. A great exercise for body control, balance, and learning math concepts.

A game that I like for balance, hand speed, and developing complex coordination and reactions is Drop and Catch. Three tennis balls are all that is needed for this game. With one ball in your child's hand, holding it palm down and shoulder high, have her drop the ball and catch it after the bounce by lowering her hand and catching it with the same hand palm up. This simple task strengthens her ability to follow instructions, agility, and speed. As she increases her ability with that hand, have her do the same thing with her other hand.

You can make the game more challenging by having her walk slowly while dropping and catching the ball, using one hand, then the other. When she is proficient at dropping and catching with each hand while walking, have her drop and catch both balls while walking. I caution not asking her to tackle a harder skill set until she is comfortable doing the basics. There are no shortcuts in learning the basics at this or any age.

This is where the third ball comes into play. While holding a ball shoulder high in each hand, place a third ball in between the balls in her hands. Have her separate her hands so the ball in the middle falls to the ground. Using only the balls in her hands, have her trap the dropped ball with a clapping motion in between the balls in her hands. This is a difficult stage of the game for all age groups. And yes, you guessed it, have her walk slowly and repeat the game. This will increase the difficulty and fun factor.

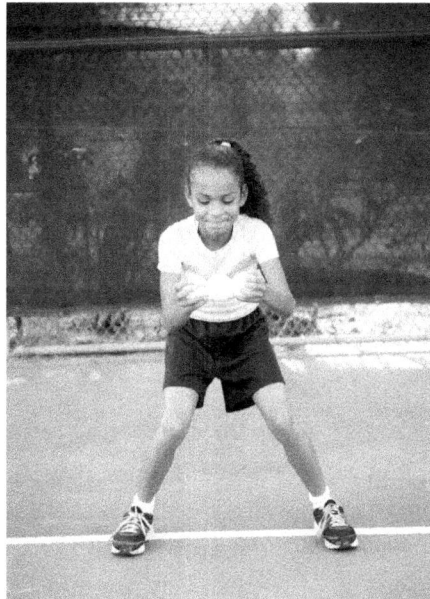

A Fun Game to Increase Coordination

Juggling balls is another fun developmental game. Start with only two balls, tossing one up in air in the direction of the dominant hand. As soon as the first ball is tossed, toss the second ball directly into the hand that tossed the first ball, and repeat the tosses. After the tossing can last thirty to sixty seconds, reverse the toss pattern. When this reverse motion becomes easier and comfortable, introduce the third ball. Holding two balls in his non-dominant hand, your child will toss one ball up in the air toward the dominant hand to be caught, and then the second ball, and then immediately toss the third ball into the non-dominant hand. Continue the toss and catch cycle.

Other activities that are good for your child's development are: hop-scotch, jumping jacks, jumping rope, squats, sit-ups, leg lifts, girls' push-ups, squat-thrusts, pull-ups, skipping, biking with a helmet on, swinging on a swing, swimming, skating, dancing, gymnastics, volley-ball, toy putt-putt golf, tumbling, supervised dodge ball, throwing and catching a ball, hula hooping, surfing, and skiing on water or snow. Games that encourage speed like Hot Potato and Hand Slap are fun to play in short durations.

Resistance training like squats, sit-ups, push-ups, pull-ups, isometrics, and using resistance bands are great natural ways to develop the body. In fact, Vincent E. "Bo" Jackson, possibly the best athlete ever to play two sports simultaneously at an elite level, did only natural resistance training through calisthenics and never lifted weights. Only a certified trainer should do weight training with children.

Playing tag is a great activity, because you need good balance to change directions. It is also important to be the chaser as well as the one chased, because of the slightly different skill sets required and developed. Unfortunately, few children in today's generation have the benefit of chasing after a squirrel, horse, dog, or chicken, as the character Rocky Balboa did in the movie Rocky.

Jumping rope and the calisthenics exercise burpees are great for developing strong healthy bodies. They are almost standalone exercises. By that, I mean that the one activity activates most of the muscle groups and gives great aerobic benefits.

Start your four-year-old off with a jump rope routine by having her hold the ends of the jump rope in her hands shoulder distance apart. Then ask her to jump over the loop of the rope that is only inches in front of her on the ground. When she clears the rope, have her move her hands to maneuver the rope over her head, placing the rope in front of her feet again.

Repeat this for a period of weeks until she jumps over the rope as soon as it hits the ground in front of her. I suggest timing her for fifteen seconds and counting the number of times that she has successful jumps. As her conditioning improves, add fifteen seconds to her durations and remember to keep track of the total jumps per time period. It makes it easy for the child to track her improvement. The physical benefits include increased muscle strength, range of motion, balance, complex coordination, and aerobic capacity. The latest research shows that jumping rope for ten minutes is the equivalent of running for twenty five to thirty five minutes.

There are different types and sizes of jump ropes from which to choose. Young children are usually afforded the basic plastic handles with a rope connected to the middle of the handle. Some ropes are made with one-inch plastic tubes around the rope from handle to handle so it swings more easily. Other ropes have ball bearings or swivels on the handle to make spinning the rope much easier.

Burpees in this age group are done by standing up straight with your hands at your side and dropping your hand down to the ground out-side your shoulders in a squat position. Simultaneously, as your hands support your body weight, kick both of your feet behind you. Then retract your feet underneath you and resume a standing position. Establish a rhythm or cadence to the exercise by counting one on the drop, two for the kick back, three for retracting your feet to the squat position, and four for the jump up. Spinning and aerobics classes utilize fast-paced music to help the participants. Counting will have a similar effect on child's rhythm. I suggest demonstrating this exercise, and then doing it alongside your child. Build a routine, with her doing two or three squat-thrusts with proper form and in two sets. As she improves, increase the number of repetitions to the first set only after she can duplicate the same number in the second set. So, if she can do four repetitions in the first set and only three in the second set, do not increase her reps in the first set yet.

A Wonderful Full Body Exercise

Let's introduce a clap above her head as she jumps up. Have her count with you as her exercise to help keep a rhythm. The next step, after she can handle all components up to this point, is to integrate a push-up. This is the first thing that she does after kicking her legs backward with both hands on the floor. With all the elements being done, the cadence is: one for the squat, two for the kick back, three for the push-up, four for the return to the squat, and five for the jump up and clap. After she can do all the elements in a good rhythm, have her add a handclap after the push-up to get the full benefits of this exercise.

With children this age, begin to introduce the concept of a shared responsibility by having them help set the table for meals. Your child will learn important lessons about where the plates, utensils, and napkins are located in the kitchen and where they are placed on the table. Memory and motor skills are enhanced while your child learns etiquette and manners. Mealtime is family time, and a good opportunity for family members to talk about their day and connect with one another.

A blessing or thanks is an activity I like to begin all family meals with. Each family member should have a chance to say the blessing on a rotating basis. During the dinner meal, I suggest playing a game called My Day. In playing My Day, each person says one or two things that he/she really enjoyed about his/her day. You can also choose to discuss one thing you liked and one thing you didn't like about your day. This engagement helps family members appreciate one another and discover things about one another that they weren't aware of.

As a child's intensity of movement increases and landing from jumping is more impactful on the body, the surface a child plays on becomes an important factor. Exercising on a beach in the sand has many benefits. The difficulty of walking in the sand helps improve balance, builds core muscles, stretches the leg muscles, and strengthens the ankles, especially when barefoot. Exercising on grass is also a preferable surface. A wooden floor is my next choice, followed by exercising on a carpet with padding. Any synthetic surface that is resilient and gives a little when landed on is a good choice. Cement, hard-surface tennis courts, and asphalt are my least favorite surfaces for high-impact workouts.

I have not mentioned stretching as part of your child's regime until now, because it is actually more technical than most people realize. A mistake that is often made is stretching first before any form of exercise. For young children, the benefits of this practice are a myth. Before a muscle is stretched, it needs an increased flow of blood. Certified trainers recommend four to eight minutes of graduated walking to jogging before stretching. The benefits of stretching for a child are increased elasticity of his body, but they do not necessarily need to stretch before exercising. It is more important to stretch after a session of high-intensity training to promote blood flow and reduce muscle cramping.

The Tracking Game is one of my favorite games. It includes spatial skills, speed, shuffling, and stopping, and offers aerobic benefits. Have your child stand in place six to ten feet opposite you. She will need ten to fifteen feet of space to shuffle to her sides. You will be holding a small ball in front of your nose. When you move the ball to the right, she will shuffle in that direction until the ball is placed in front of your nose. Use verbal keys of "shuffle" and "stop" to assist her at first. The rhythm of the movement of the ball should match her ability to start and stop. Vary the ball movement from left to right and right to left. When she is comfortable with that pattern, increase the difficulty of the game by changing the pattern to repeating the previous movement. After she is comfortable with starting from a standing stop position, have her jog in place whenever the ball is in front of your nose. This will also increase the fun factor. This is a great game for her to play with a sibling or a neighbor.

Don't Forget Free Play

Unstructured play or free play has the value of physical and creative development. Whether playing alone or with others, their development is not on a holiday. Children start playing either with parents or by themselves. If you have only one child, may I suggest that you play with your child and teach sharing before introducing your child to another child. It will help in this inevitable issue with young children. If there is a special toy that your child likes, don't take it out when others come over to play.

A well-equipped and well-designed playground has a world of benefits for a young child's physical and cognitive development. In our summer camp, I take my tennis students ages four to eight to an adjoining playground every day as a treat and to explore the wonders of free play. Not only do they enjoy playing on the equipment, but create games to play with one another in this exciting environment.

The next chapter addresses activities with a higher degree of difficulty and benefits for your child.

CHAPTER EIGHT
Parent Teaching – Stage Three

Challenging and Fun Activities and Games

The training ladder is a great basic tool for movement with young children and professional athletes alike. Ladders come in different lengths and construction design. Choose a ten- to eighteen-foot ladder. I like a longer ladder because a short ladder is quickly obsolete with an active child. Some ladders have adjustable rungs that can be problematic, because they can move quite easily when jumped on during use. I find that fixed rungs work better in most applications. The other variable is the shape of the rungs. You're better off choosing flat rungs for safety, as elevated rungs can cause twisted ankles or serious injury.

The first game that I suggest is called the Bunny Hop. Have your child start in front of the first rung and hop into the first square. Then inch up to the second rung before trying to jump into the second square. Now demonstrate this for your child so he will understand the concept.

A Great Balance and Coordination Exercise

The key to this game is the use of the arms and legs. Your child should look like a standing broad jumper, hopping from one square to another. Your child must come to a complete stop before hopping to the next square, as this helps develop balance. The rhythm of hopping and stopping will contribute to improved leg and core muscle strength, body control, and, most importantly, your child will have a lot of fun. When proficiency is evident, set his goal to jump over one square, then increase the number of squares by one as his ability increases.

The Backward Bunny game is hopping backward in the ladder using the same teaching steps used to play the Bunny game. The one exception is this game allows the participant to hop as many times as needed to go through each square. Going backward should not be done with the body in the upright position or standing tall position. When going backward, the head and shoulders should be leaning forward, knees slightly bent, and the butt should be in a sitting position. This is the correct position for all ages to move backward quickly and safely. Do not try to jump any more than one square at a time while hopping backward. This game is difficult for anyone, because we seldom travel backward, except in sports.

A great game for balance is called the Egyptian Walk. Starting with both feet together, have your child lift either knee even with her belly button and hold for two seconds. Then have her turn that knee outward as far as she can, but not moving her hips. After a two-second hold, she should return her knee in front of her and step forward. She repeats this movement with the other leg until she goes to the end of the line or ladder. As her balance improves, increase the seconds of the holds. This makes balancing more difficult. As mentioned before, progress will be slow. After she becomes proficient going forward with good form, have her do it going backward.

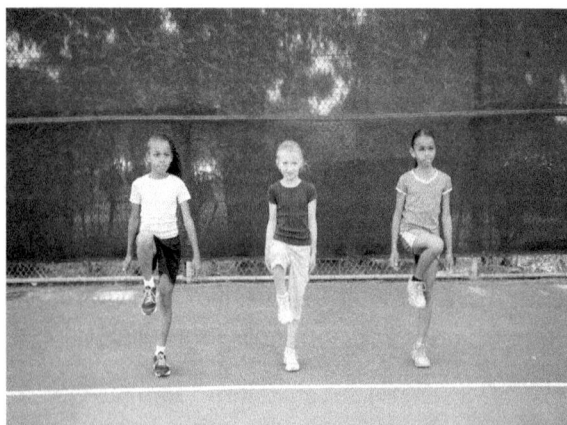

Develops Balance and Core Strength

The next games are the Right Foot Hops and Left Foot Hops. Your child uses only the right or left foot, one at a time, and hops through the ladder. They are simple games, but with a plethora of benefits. In time, when your child's skill set improves, you can ask him to do the hops going backward.

You can increase your child's spatial skills by tossing him a ball or beanbag while he's hopping through the ladder. After catching the ball, allow him to hop a few times and then ask him to toss the ball underhand back to you. Do not forget the verbal approval of telling him "nice catch" if he catches the ball or "nice try" if he does not. If the ball tossed by you is too hard to catch, say, "my bad," letting him know that you did not toss the ball well.

At first his tosses may be wild and hard to catch. Reward him verbally with "nice toss" if the toss is good. Use a key word that represents you asking him to toss the ball back to you. I like to use a word that he chooses, like chocolate, banana, or ice cream as a signal for him to toss the ball back. Having him choose a word creates more buy-in to "his" game. If he is having trouble tossing the ball to you, notice when he tosses it. Is it after he lands or simultaneous when he hops? Encourage him to toss the ball to you when he is stopped. His balance will be better when he is stopped.

The Sideways Hopping game is hopping sideways with both feet, starting from the outside of the first square into the first square and continuing all the way to the outside of the last square. Then reverse the hopping in the opposite direction. The keys to this game are the balance in the hops, control in landing, and building a rhythm in hops with arm swings.

The Ladder Shuffle game starts at one end of the ladder and goes through the ladder to the other end. Your child will shuffle by using her lead foot, followed by her other foot, into each square until she is at the opposite end. Then reverse the shuffle in the opposite direction. It's important that your child has her knees slightly bent for good balance.

The In and Out game requires your child to hop with both feet into the first square and hop out to the right of the ladder, then into the next square, continuing to the end. Have her turn around and face the direction that she came from, and do the game by hopping to the left of the square until she travels through the ladder. The final progression of the game is to hop into the first square, hop out to the right, back into the next square, then hop out to the left. Continue this in-and-out pattern for the length of the ladder.

The Footstep game is the most difficult to master for most children. It entails starting on the left side of the first square and stepping into the square with her right foot, followed by her left foot. She will now step into the square that she is next to with her right foot, followed by her left foot. With her right foot, she will step out and up to the next square, followed by her left foot. She will continue through the ladder, crossing from side to side using her right foot as her lead step. The Left Footstep game follows the same pattern, but with the left foot as the lead foot.

A Great Brain and Movement Development Game

CONES

Children love the use of cones to promote change of direction and change of speed. Cones are also a fun birthday party activity for all ages. My favorite is the Five Cone game. Place three cones two feet apart on a parallel line and two cones three feet apart on another parallel line. Starting on the outside of cone number one, run forward and around cone two, then backward behind cone three, then forward and around cone four, and backward to the outside of cone five. Timing a child in this game is fun and shows his progress as he learns to maneuver through the cones.

A Pattern for Fun and Serious Training

The Ice Cream game is also a fun use of cones. With your child holding the top of the cone in his hand and the bottom up, toss a ball in the air for him to catch in the bottom of the cone. Vary the distance of the toss to increase difficulty and the fun factor.

ACTION GAMES

Catch Me is played with at least two children. Space two children two to three feet apart with a cone for each to stand by. Place a third cone ten feet away for a target for the first child. Start both children running at the same time. The child behind the child closest to the cone is trying to touch the child in front of him/her. This is a great game to time; keep a record to track improvement. For accuracy, ensure that the distances of the cones are the same in all games, so that you compare the same distances run.

The Bridge Game is played on a hard surface, with a child standing with his legs apart facing a barrier ten to twenty feet away. A ball is tossed between his legs from behind so he doesn't know when it's being tossed. The moment he sees the ball, he runs after it and stops it. This game is great for developing quickness, tracking, and anticipation. To work on his perceptual speed, toss the ball at varying rates of speed.

Circle the Ball is a great game for aerobic and footwork development. Simply toss a small ball at a slow rate of speed and have your child run and circle the ball as it rolls until it stops. Change the rate of speed of the toss and the direction that she circles the ball as she improves her skills.

Remember the game in chapter 6, called Caterpillar? It features two or more children standing one behind the other with their feet shoulder distance apart. Balls are rolled and the children have to move so the ball goes between their feet. When the ball touches a foot, that child moves to the back of the group and is the tail. Once played it is never forgotten!

Repetition and consistency are needed to reinforce how a movement is performed. Your child will develop a sense of the correct motion through trial and error. When the motion is performed correctly, the child will try to repeat this feeling. That is why many coaches ask the question, "How does that feel?"

For children six and older, the ability to feel the physical mechanics of correct movement will help in his awareness and ability to self-correct.

The value of good coaching is to make sure that a child is aware of the mechanics of correct movement. Then, and only then, can self-correction occur. Most elite coaches would rather a child hit twenty out of twenty balls correctly, than hit one hundred balls only hitting eighty correctly. Practice for each child should be geared to that child's own level of perfection. Proper mechanics will also help prevent injury.

Circuit training is a great form of exercise for young children and helps avoid boredom. Too many of us do the same set of exercises routinely, which actually restricts our potential fitness and conditioning. When creating a good circuit for your child, make sure there are components of upper and lower body, core strength, and aerobic conditioning. Also rotate the components so your child doesn't overwork any one area during her workouts.

As excited as I am to see parents become dual-goal coaches, I do have concerns when it comes to coaching your child in sports. Almost every day I see parents going beyond their knowledge and abilities working with their children in sports. I see parents teaching their child a technique that is either incorrect or incomplete. Even the top professional trainers and coaches confer with others to confirm their coaching practices and beliefs. On the other hand, I have seen many good professional coaches be extremely successful coaching their own children. So it can be done. If you aren't confident in the skill you are teaching, let a professional work with your child.

No matter what activity a child is involved in, the most important factor is that he is having fun. If it is not fun, the activity will not be sustained. This is true for adult activities as well.

Playing with your child will help develop her cognitive and athletic potential. It also will help you build a more intimate lifetime bond with your child. Childhood is much too short for both the child and the parent. Although we all have wondered when the frustrating parts of parenthood will end, these childhood years are really so brief and must be savored. Raising young children is a wonderful time of discovery and appreciation for the things that really matter in life—family. It's never too late to play games or sports with your child or grandchild.

CHAPTER NINE
Selecting Your Child's Initial Activities and Sports

In this chapter, I suggest activities and sports that I feel will be beneficial for your child's physical development in the short term, and for a lifetime of benefits if continued. If you have already taken advantage of working with your child as described in chapters 6, 7, and 8, you will have a better idea which sports are a good fit for your child. You will know firsthand, having worked with your child in strengthening his balance, spatial, attention, and movement skills.

If you have not had the opportunity to practice these developmental activities with your child, start today. It's never too late to start. In fact, almost every sport is dependent on the ability to be proficient in the basic skills that were taught in previous chapters. These activities will greatly improve your child's abilities and will prepare your child for a physically active life.

Activities to Develop _Fun_damentals and the Fun of Competition
The foundation for competitive and athletic prowess can start between the ages of one and a half and four years old. This is a time when the

less than graceful child begins to learn more complex body movement. Parents can foster the right competitive spirit in their child by recognizing and rewarding a child's efforts in trying to acquire any new physical skill. Rewarding effort is crucial in motivating a child to continue learning and excelling. Rewarding your child verbally for his effort is positive reinforcement that can easily be adapted to all aspects of your child's endeavors.

Start off by doing a short walking race with your child. Sometimes you can allow her to beat you, while other times tying or beating her. Reward your child's effort if it's good, no matter how he/she does in the race. This rewarding effort will go a long way in learning to handle failure in the future. Also, not letting your child win all the time will heighten his/her ability to cope with failure. A caution here: do not reward your child for a poor effort. Let your child know that she either can or has done better. Children know the difference, and if they don't know at this age, you will be teaching them a good lesson.

Competition, if fun, will inspire her desire to improve her performance. That will be a great attribute for your child's entire life. Use the same process with your child in running. This simple process of rewarding effort verbally will implant a healthy competitive nature in your child and help her cope with failure. Your child's desire to improve will lead to her developing a strong work ethic. It does not get any better in parenting when you plant the behavioral seeds and watch your child excel. Make sure that your expectations of your child remain realistic in each developmental stage.

Be patient with your child in terms of your expectations. Your child can sense your frustration if he/she fails to meet your expectations. Your frustration can send unconscious messages to your child. These could very likely cause your child to quit a sport or activity that he/she really enjoys. Why? At this age, your child wants to please you. If you are unhappy, your child will tend to be unhappy. Children do not want to suffer from your disapproval. Your child reads your facial expressions, tone of voice, and body language—oftentimes as well as an FBI profiler.

Walking and running are important for your child's coordination, balance, and aerobic benefit. Children in today's world have a tremendous lack of aerobic training because of the reduced amount of after-school play. I suggest introducing interval training as presented in chapter 7. Additional benefits will be generated if both walking and running are done in the sand at the beach. And being barefoot in the sand offers the added benefits of stretching and strengthening the muscles and tendons in the feet, toes, ankles, and legs. The sand allows for more flexibility, resistance, and an increased aerobic workout. If sand is not available, a workout in a grassy playground or large backyard will be fine. Barefoot exercising is always beneficial on most surfaces. Just be cautious of surfaces that may have sharp objects.

Notice that I used the term workout in the last paragraph. Using the word workout often when you exercise with your child could leave him with the idea that working out is a normal activity to be performed throughout his lifetime. Too many adults relate workout to a sport. My message here is that exercise should be part of everyone's lifestyle as long as one is able.

Traversing a levee or small hill is also advantageous in the development of balance, strength, and endurance. While at the playground or someone's backyard, use the swing set to energize your child's imagination, muscles, and balance. Few things beat that feeling of acceleration into the wind, the rush of energy in your body, or the breathtaking ride to the top of the swing's arches.

A child overcoming the fear of water being splashed in his face teaches a good lesson. The transition from fear to fun is rewarding for both child and parent. Even the old school rubber ducky in the bathtub will increase coordination and motor skills as your child reaches for and squeezes the ducky. This exposure to water can lead a child to an early start in swimming, which is a good skill for health and survival.

I rank swimming right up there with gymnastics for a young child to learn and become athletically competent and confident. Swimming is a great health tool because it can be performed for a lifetime. I cannot think of another sport or activity that has equal health benefits. A swimmer develops general strength, cardio fitness, and endurance. There are also the psychological benefits of being able to relax and swim with little effort while doing laps. Swimmers usually leave their sessions refreshed, as opposed to being mentally and physically exhausted. Lap swimming and distance running develop the habit of deep breathing. We naturally breathe too shallow, especially when our muscles are tight. Having been a competitive swimmer and coach myself, I have seen the many benefits of swimming for all age groups. When the weather permits, I still swim two to three times a week for my pleasure and health.

Developmental stages cannot be rushed and put on our timetable. Each child, even in the same gene pool, may differ in ability, motivation, competitive personality, and athletic skill levels. An example of this is a tennis player who competed in junior age groups and was ranked only 145 in the world. Most world-class legends in the juniors are ranked in the top ten to fifteen. He became a Grand Slam winner and former number-one player. His name is Rafael "Rafa" Nadal. As a junior, Rafael was a good soccer player.

My second example is of a high school basketball player who was cut from the team as a sophomore. The next year he made the team and played well enough to earn a scholarship to play for University of North Carolina's Tar Heels. He went to the professional ranks to become possibly the best basketball player of all time. His name is Michael "Air" Jordan. Some children are slow starters in many areas of life. Michael's second sport as a child was baseball, which he also played at the professional level.

Continual positive reinforcement is the key to creating a secure environment for your child. Sometimes as parents, we sabotage our children by not catching them and recognizing their good deeds and behavior. Since their negative behavior is against our wills, parents often overreact when angry. Remember that your children's thoughts lead them to their actions. So do not just focus on their actions, drill down and analyze the thought process that leads to that undesirable behavior.

Several decades ago I read a great management book, The One-Minute Manager, by Dr. Kenneth H. Blanchard and Spencer Johnson. The theme of the book was to acknowledge employees doing positive things. This is a great lesson for parents to consider for their child. Positive comments fill a child's emotional tank and balance the constructive criticism that may be taken negatively by your child. Negative comments have the tendency to deplete one's emotional tank. I don't advise you to become a helicopter parent, but to find a balance of giving corrective comments in a positive manner.

Many sports and physical instructional programs focus on practicing over and over what a child does well. The logic behind this may be explained by today's pampering world, in which a child needs to always feel good about the activity that he/she is doing. The thought seems to be predicated on a false fear that children will quit if they are challenged or experience failure. Consequently, the same lesson is repeated time and again to the point that affects improvement.

This type of program produces activities that pale in value to an instructional process that reviews each previous lesson and introduces new materials to promote growth and stimulation. Over-teaching one area of a sport or activity often occurs because of the teacher's lack of skill. Coaches must have a thorough understanding of the rudiments of a sport and have the ability to explain and demonstrate those fundamentals. Further, they must be able to communicate and recognize the learning preferences of each child to maximize each student's talents and efforts. A coach is responsible for encouraging and igniting the fire to be competitive while having fun. My point is, coaches have a platform to make sports fun or frightening.

I suggest continuing with all the activities previously mentioned for children ages four to six. Focus on the activities that present both difficulty and fun for your child. Consider family trips to museums for exercise and culture. Visit nearby farms to learn how our food is raised or grown, frequent parks and playgrounds for old-fashioned picnics. Take advantage of canoeing for exercise and teaching water safety. Do not forget to take your child fishing because it provides as opportunity for many teachable and fun moments. Pony rides can be great, especially for a child who does not normally have access to large animals.

Don't forget to have regular picture-taking sessions everywhere your family goes. Display these pictures in your child's room, on the refrigerator, and elsewhere for regular viewing. Pictures are a wonderful source of memories for everyone, including relatives and friends. Grandparents will cherish any picture of their grandchild.

Go on weekly family bike rides around the block or in a park. For safety reasons, if your child is in the beginning stages of riding, perhaps to walk or run alongside your child would be best. Safety in bike riding also requires the wearing of a certified helmet in most states. I see too many parents not wearing helmets, either because of the expense or because they do not see the need. I lost a friend whose head hit a mailbox while he was riding his bike and he died from the accident. Parents wearing their helmets will be good role models for their children.

I personally think that if a child can learn to ride a bike with training wheels, it's a lot better than riding a tricycle. The ergonomics of a bike with training wheels offer a preferable position for them than does being seated on a tricycle. The challenge of balancing is greater on the bike with training wheels. A child with good balance will quickly outgrow a tricycle.

The three-wheeler does afford a steady base that allows a child to easily ride in a chair-like seated position while learning how to steer and pedal. Depending on your child's physical strength and ability, a tricycle may be a good choice. A disadvantage of a tricycle is that you will have to deal with the expense, storage, and disposal in a short period of time.

Consider your child starting to do biathlons at the age of three years old. Combine two activities like walking and running for their first official biathlon event. You set the distance and the rules. Add riding a tricycle or biking to the mix for variety. After your child can swim even one lap in a pool, challenge her with a triathlon comprised of a swim, a bike ride, and a run. Again, you set the distances and the rules. You will find that your child will enjoy picking events to be incorporated into his/her multi-sport events.

Sports involvement for your four- to six-year-old child that I suggest would be to continue with swimming and gymnastics. Parents typically pick the sport that their young child plays. Some parents pick team sports because they think these offer the value of teamwork for a common goal. However, being responsible and accountable for improvement is often less evident in team sports than in the early stages of individual sports. I caution you not to determine your child's involvement in sports by your involvement or noninvolvement. Poor experiences in sports are often caused by poor programs or coaches, not the sport.

Parents should be aware that for a young child to be successful in sports, or anything for that matter, he/she must have listening skills. The inability to listen makes children almost impossible to teach. Next is the ability to focus and give 100 percent effort to learn and execute the required mechanics. And for children eight years old and older, learning to commit to practice time is important in order to achieve goals.

What I hear sometimes from young children who are involved in team sports is that they are doing well, but some of their teammates are weak. This is often an obvious excuse for a child's poor performance and shortcomings. Other times, it is a fair assessment, and if it's accurate, it may build frustration rather than teamwork in that child who is far better than his peers.

Individual sports hone a child's sense of responsibility because he/she is dependent on his/her own skills and actions. Through individual sports, self-determination and motivation are illuminated. Tennis, golf, table tennis, skiing, running, swimming, and diving are great choices of individual sports for a child.

Horseback riding is also a great activity and sport for a child. It's an even more meaningful activity if a child learns to help take care of the animal. Few sports afford a child the opportunity to learn responsibility better than the daily care of a horse.

I grew up riding, rode bareback at the age of eight, and had my first horse when I was fourteen. After taking riding lessons, I competed in horse shows for a year riding English saddle. As an adult, I played polo for the Hilton Head Polo Club and had four horses, a truck, and a trailer.

And for a year, I enjoyed team-penning cows riding Western. I miss being around horses and being able to ride.

All sports can teach wonderful life lessons. Even though I predominantly teach individual sports, I value the lessons that team sports have to offer. In my tennis lessons with four- to ten-year-olds, I divide the class into two groups. I have each group choose a name for their team before they start group competition. Being able to choose their own name helps them become more invested in the team process. This also offers a lesson in understanding how a team must build consensus to make decisions. Players learn to recognize and respect the opinion of everyone on the team. This process will also break the habit of a child saying, "I want" anytime that he/she wants something in a group setting.

The value of this team competition is also to create a setting in which each child will benefit. Each child will be taught not to blame a weaker child for not doing well, but to support the other child. I enjoy teaching a child that, by making fewer mistakes, he will score more points and perform better as a team member. This lesson serves a child in every aspect of his life.

Parent Traps
Parents frequently fall into the "quitting" trap when their child is in a multi-week or multi-month lesson. After you do your due diligence in researching a sport or program, include your child in the final decision. Explain to your child that both you and he are committing to this program for the full term. This will help teach proper decision making and commitment. Allowing the child to quit is a disservice to him, his teammates, the coaches, and your finances. Allowing him to quit also sets the stage for him to quit anything he wishes in the future. The only exception is if the program is flawed or has a poor coaching role model.

You can avoid other traps if you:

- Analyze sports based on your child's personality and current skill set level.

- Choose sports that your child has showed interest in.

- Look at both the time commitment for you and your child to be involved in the sport.

- Check how it will affect other family commitments.

- Consider how much playing and practice time will be available to your child in each program.

- Check the coach-to-child ratio.

- Check the coach's teaching qualifications and certifications.

- Observe a coach's abilities in teaching groups and private lessons.

- Consider your child's ability to learn with the coaching style used.

- Is the program a fundamentals builder or just an activity?

- Understand that a child who specializes in one sport is more susceptible to stress injuries.

- Is the coaching focus on the individual's performance or is it on the team's performance?

- Check the cost of lessons, equipment, travel, and incidentals for each sport.

- Will your child be able to find pickup games to continue playing the sport short and long term?

- Is the sport an activity that your family can play?

- Does the program that you are considering fit your child's needs?

Other Parent Tips

Take the opportunity to watch a variety of sporting events with your child. In person is often the best, but watching sports on TV will also work. Tell her in advance what time the game is on so you don't pull her away from something else that she has her heart set on doing. Take the time to explain some of the rules of play and the object of the game. Ask her for her opinion of the game. Make it fun and have her favorite snack during the game. Do not expect her to watch the entire game. When you sense that she has seen enough, give her a hug and thank her for watching with you. She may stay a little longer or leave right away. In either case, she has some control. This will set the stage for another sports date with your child.

When your child is aware of what is going on in a game, comment on the flashy shots or plays made by some of the players. They look exciting, and a child will try to emulate them when he plays. Make it a great teaching opportunity, and explain that a flashy shot is usually a low-percentage shot and is often missed. Take the opportunity to reinforce that consistent play and making fewer mistakes than your opponent wins games. You will find many teachable moments while watching sports with your child.

After your child is enrolled in any program, ask the coach to suggest activities that you can do with your child to reinforce the lessons or speed up your child's learning curve. From personal experience as a coach, I appreciate when parents are so interested in their child that they will spend time playing with him/her. Think of it as helping children with their sports homework. I encourage parents to watch their child's lessons so they use similar verbiage to what the coach uses.

Tennis is a great sport to introduce to a child in this age group. Tennis encourages spatial skills and general complex coordination. Proper training involves teaching the volley first, since it can be learned in a few minutes, along with the overhead. A child being able to hit the ball over the net in a short period of time builds self-confidence and ignites the fun factor. It's not fun for anyone to struggle when he/she is learning something new. Children and adults alike get frustrated and bored very easily if they are unable to perform a specific activity.

Having fun is one of the most important factors for a person's emotional state of mind. If a child has fun during the training process, he will continue the sport. It further heightens the sheer excitement of competition. After the competition, a child learns to reset his goals and focuses more energy on training.

Being a developmental tennis coach, I unequivocally believe that a portion of the beginning of each lesson needs to include specific complex-coordination, spatial, reaction, and balance drills. The purpose of teaching these skills is not only to help play tennis, but for any sport a child may play in the future. These exercises are also great for your child's physical and mental well-being. Many games and activities were mentioned in previous chapters to start with your child from two to ten years old.

The activity that tops my list for a child to learn is swimming. As a child's skill sets improve, I feel that he/she should learn two to three of the four competitive strokes. Not that every child should be a competitive swimmer, but it's important to learn technique for efficiency in the water. The four strokes are, in order of progression: freestyle, backstroke, breaststroke, and butterfly. When properly taught to this age group, kids will benefit by not only being able to swim, but also by learning water safety, gaining a sense of confidence, and increasing aerobic development.

The simple activity of your child taking a deep breath, closing his/her mouth, and going under water while you count is a good game. You are counting to measure the amount of time that your child can hold his breath underwater. A child feels more secure in doing this if he can touch the bottom of the pool and if you are lightly holding his trunk.

Verbally congratulate your child when he's able to do any new activity. Acknowledging his improvement, no matter how slight, encourages him to do even better. However, when your child does not do as well as in previous attempts, let him know how he did. It's always better if the session ends on a positive note at this age. A child will remember that success the next time you engage in playing that game.

Our lives are filled with competition. There is competition in school, academics, athletics, for clubs we may want to join, and for social acceptance. Later in life we face the intense competition for jobs. And in the workplace, we find constant competition to keep our jobs. So why not develop the work ethic, effort, and focus needed to compete at an early age? We are in the game of life, whether we like it or not.

At seven to eight years old, I would encourage a child to try basketball, which builds skills necessary for all athletic pursuits. Do yourself and your child a favor by teaching him how to dribble the age-appropriate ball with either hand before you enroll him in a class. Kids will benefit by learning to handle the ball. Also, if they do not seem to adapt to dribbling, perhaps wait three to six months before enrolling in basketball. Oftentimes, starting a child in a sport before his skill sets are developed sets him up for failure in that sport.

Make sure to buy the proper sports equipment for your child. I see too many children with a parent's racket that is heavy and too long for them. If a child plays basketball and does not have one, how will he practice? Whatever the sport, children's interest will grow exponentially when they have "their own" equipment. It helps them become more invested in the sport and allows them to practice with other children.

Track and field sports such as running and jumping are great athletic skill builders for children. With the cutbacks in many schools' physical education programs, track is not offered as much as it was in my era. In fact, the New Orleans Recreation Department would semiannually sponsor track and field meets at playgrounds throughout the city with competition in various age groups. We didn't have to win to have fun. Just to participate was fun. A highlight for many of us was to enter an age group above ours. It was especially fun if we could beat a few of the older kids.

Your child could try a junior golf clinic, again, only if his/her coordination warrants the challenge. Soccer is a possible choice if the child has good balance and can start, stop, and change directions quickly. Being able to kick the ball with either foot is important. If children do not have these skill sets to some degree already, they may lose interest in the sport quickly. Playing kickball with a child four years or older helps prepare her for soccer and other sports as well.

Where you live is also a factor in choosing a sport. Obviously, if you live in a mountainous area, snow skiing could be an option. If you live close to a lake or ocean, sailing, surfing, or water-skiing might be interesting for your child. So be creative here. I like sports that are age- and skill-set-appropriate for any child. Sport involvement should be challenging to all the muscle groups, but not be overwhelming to the child. My favorite sports are those that require both mental and physical skills and can be played through adulthood. Wait until your child has attained the basic skills before enrolling him/her in a sports program. This can easily be done if you participate in the program offered in chapters 7 and 8. However, if your child is five years old and has phenomenal skill sets, along with the right temperament, no sport is off-limits.

Baseball can be a good sport if your child excels in focus and can handle periods of less stimulation. There can be a lot of sitting and standing around to contend with in this sport, which can be especially difficult for a young child and his/her parents.

Sports are also enjoyed by millions of people who don't actually play them. Many enjoy the pleasure of sports in the Summer and Winter Olympics, which are a great source of entertainment and national pride. This is also true of World Cup Soccer and other sports on a worldwide platform.

The challenge of not having the full complement of skill sets for a sport shows up in high school. Often, a freshman in high school will try out for a sport that he/she has not played. Most of the time, students have friends on a team or a parent urging them to play. They go to tryouts to make a competitive team that has a limited roster to fill. At the high school level, I will bet that more than 99 percent of the kids who go out for teams have been playing that sport for three to six years. In high school, for the school's reputation, student body, and coach, it is all about winning. High school is not the setting to start a new sport. Club teams or recreation teams are a much better platform for beginners in high school. If your child is both physically talented and motivated to play a sport, there are few boundaries to playing any sport, even with a late start.

As previously mentioned, I don't agree with the concept of a young child playing a game without the score being kept. In fact, I insist that all players in both individual and team games know the score.

The responsibility of each player keeping score goes to the core of a full understanding of any game. This understanding illuminates the reasons for success and the reasons for failure. Failure helps us identify specific aspects of our game that are causing us not to be successful. Then attention can be given to practicing our weakness necessary to improve performance.

Without a measure of accomplishment, when does a child learn to set goals and have that euphoric feeling of accomplishment? Start your child's goal setting at around three to four years of age. This will go a long way in establishing study habits, plus coping with failure and success. If you believe in giving your children an allowance for just being, I suggest that you rethink this issue. Picking up their toys and keeping their room livable is their responsibility. Consider giving rewards for doing extra chores.

Karate, as a sport and a discipline, has many benefits for participants of all ages. It can be a great in-depth physical and mental conditioner, more so than some other sports, because proficiency in karate gives one a feeling of self-confidence and the security of personal well-being that can transcend far beyond the sport. That confidence can manifest itself in all area of a child's life. It can, however, take four to six years in the proper program to attain this euphoric state of mind. It's not just a feeling that you can physically defend yourself, but provides peace of mind and a sense of calm in your consciousness.

While visiting South Korea some years ago, I realized that karate is taught to all schoolchildren. It made quite an impression to watch boys and girls of all ages learning the sport of discipline and mental and physical control.

In the nine to ten age group, all sports are fair game: volleyball, surfing, football, triathlons, sailing, ice hockey, lacrosse, table tennis, etc. The exception, at this age, is weight training. Most sports experts point to the development of a child's growth plates as a barrier to heavy lifting at an early age.

Old-fashioned calisthenics are a natural body development tool for any child at this age, as mentioned in chapter 7. Many calisthenic exercises provide weight training because they involve moving and lifting one's own body weight. Unfortunately, the calisthenics that are needed at this level are rarely available to children, except through participation with a personal trainer. The value of calisthenics cannot be overstated.

An example of what calisthenics can do for an athlete is found in a Georgia-born athlete who did them throughout his well-documented career. He began his program at the age of twelve and still practices it to this day. In the first year, he performed one hundred thousand push-ups and one hundred thousand sit-ups. He led his high school football team with eighty-six touchdowns in four years and was an A student. He was a standout in track and field in high school and college. He was a three-time All-American in football and won the coveted Heisman Trophy in 1982. He had a great career as a professional football player and earned a fifth-degree black belt in tae kwon do. He competed in the 1992 Olympics in the two-man bobsled, finishing seventh. His name is Herschel J. Walker.

Certified developmental coaches and trainers will tell you that just playing a sport or several sports will not provide the strength and flexibility needed to perform at a higher competitive level. Simply put, coaches focus on the techniques and playing of their sport, while trainers focus on developing the muscles that preform the mechanics of sports. That is why many top high school and most college athletes have strength and conditioning sessions as part of their normal regimen. Unfortunately, it seems that the perception of calisthenics for children is not appreciated by today's generation of parents.

Missed Opportunities

After a child begins a sport, parents tend to have one or several common missed opportunities. The first involves a child's practice times. Many parents do not take advantage of their child's playing and practicing with other children or a parent. For children six years old, playing a sport with another child, whether supervised by an adult or unsupervised, can be very beneficial. When playing with a friend, children quickly discover the need to learn the game's rules and improve their skills. It also strengthens the experiences of fun and fellowship.

Children need more practice time, not necessarily more lessons. Otherwise, children are being taught how to take lessons, without actually ever playing the game. That being said, the use of improper technique will limit a child's improvement. There needs to be a good balance of lessons and practice time. Ask your child's coach to recommend specific practice suggestions to ensure your child's improvement and success in a sport.

It seems like today's culture in most sports has changed from a child playing with another child to ongoing private or semiprivate sport lessons. Even parents who play sports misunderstand this opportunity.

The second parent-missed opportunity is choosing a single sport in which his/her child should specialize. For a young child, this is not a good idea. I have seen time and time again a child specializing in one sport for three to six years, then quitting that sport and not playing any other sport. For children, sports are an opportunity to socialize with friends, release energy, and just have fun. Many of the world's top athletes use a second or third sport to relax and play merely for fun.

On the premise that you have taught your child the games and activities in this book and developed their coordination, complex coordination, body movement, and spatial skills, they should be prepared for almost any sport. The child just needs the proper coaching and interest to play to the best of her abilities.

The third missed opportunity is the enormous lack of sport periodization that is very common today. Periodization is dividing any sport into three equally valuable periods.

- The preparatory period focuses on specific and general preparation in physical, technique, tactical, and mental areas of the sport.

- The next period is the competition season and championship season in which athletes exhibit their best performances.

- The transition period is when athletes take their psychological, physical, and relaxation breaks. The optimal duration for this phase is two to three weeks.

Without the transition or rest stage, an athlete is susceptible to physical injury and mental fatigue. A young child who plays in pain could be risking his future with a permanent disability. Mental fatigue will not only affect sports performance. Mental fatigue can affect a child's grades, behavior, and eating habits. One's entire life is affected by judgments made without the benefit of clear thinking.

There are entirely too many children who play one sport for twelve months without a break. There are also too many children who play several sports year-round without taking advantage of the transition or rest stage.

A basic guideline is for youths to practice only the number of hours a week as their age. So, a child of six should practice no more than six hours a week. Practicing more hours than their age may lead to severe overuse injuries. This is most commonly found with young pitchers in baseball. The pressure to excel by throwing faster pitches and curve-balls can distort joints and muscles.

A coach's note: Picking up your child from school and rushing him/her to lessons without a snack break is difficult on your child and the coach. Remember to give your child a snack, which will invariably give the coach a more receptive student.

Now, let's focus on how to select a coach for your child.

CHAPTER TEN
Selecting Coaches for Your Child

———

Selecting a developmental coach for your young child could be a simple task, depending on your expectations and limitations. Some parents select coaches simply based on the day and time a carpool is available. Other parents select a coach based on who coaches their next-door neighbor's child. Distance to the teaching facility from their home also heads many parents' lists. Expense of the classes is another important factor in parents' selection. All these selection prerequisites are valid concerns.

A question that I ask you to consider for any activity is, "What are your expected outcomes of your child's time spent in this class?" And, "How does this program fit into your overall developmental vision for your child?" If it's just to fill a void in his/her weekly activity schedule or for the class to act as a sitter for you, please skip to the next chapter!

I suggest that you consider the following guidelines, particularly in determining your child's first coach. First, seek out a seasoned coach who relates well to your child's age group and skill level, and is a positive role model on and off the court. Seek a dual-goal coach who will teach not only the sport, but life lessons as well. Consider a coach who is active and certified in his sport or profession's organization to teach children. The coach should exhibit knowledge of the mechanics needed to teach your child and be able to transition him to the next level of competency in the sport. The coach's sense of humor is also important for a child in this age group. Humor keeps a child engaged and focused on the lesson.

In researching the correct coach for your child, do the obvious and ask other parents why they recommend a certain coach. Drill down deep and ask for specific examples of the positives and negatives. Remember that each parent is somewhat invested in his/her child's coach. Look for some passion in the reasons they recommend a specific coach.

The candidate should have the ability to teach your child to play, understand the game, and improve all skill sets. Then the intangibles of teaching decision-making skills, tactics, focus, goal setting, self-evaluation, and life lessons can be applied to the sport, but also incorporated into other aspects of their lives. And, by the way, many life lessons can be taught at varying levels to four- to eight-year-olds. You would be amazed at the number of teachable moments a dual-goal coach can find in a once-a-week hour-long lesson that will positively impact a child. Many coaches enjoy a platform of respect that enables them to immediately be in a position of authority and a positive role model for your child. They do this through their personality and adaptive communication style.

Watch a practice session or two of any prospective coach. You may want to watch with your child and spouse. I personally like both parents to be in on the decision making, especially if the parents are legally separated or divorced. For parents who are separated or divorced, I frequently find that one parent may be passionate about the lessons and the other has no buy-in and may not support the activity when he/she has custody. The child suffers because he/she misses the lessons and realizes that one parent cares more about his/her own agenda than about the child's development.

It's important to examine the level of discipline of both the coach and the students. Do the students listen to the coach, does the coach listen to them, is the coach respectful to all members of the class, and is the class safe and fun for everyone? Some coaches are great in a private session and are lost in a group lesson.

A competent coach can give each child in his/her class the individual attention that is required for individuals to learn new skills. A seasoned coach uses scalability in teaching a group, which allows for each child's athletic and learning ability. So a child who has advanced motor skills will be challenged by the coach expecting his/her technique to be better or executed with more accuracy than a child with less developed skills.

Furthermore, a good coach can quickly evaluate each child's best learning style and employ that technique to aid in the learning process. A coach employing scalability in teaching differs greatly from a coach teaching predominantly to the top students or teaching to the middle of the class's skill level, which is often the case. A coach teaching the whole class to the pace of the slower learners is not acceptable. Children become quickly bored and will not like that a certain segment of the class is getting more attention, nor will the parents.

Lessons should replicate the intensity of real games and be fun. Fun is the glue that makes learning sports something very special to children. Ensure that the teacher-to-student ratio allows the time needed by your child to stay interested and engaged. Coaches have different abilities in teaching. The number of children in a class should match the teacher's skill level. Observe your child's coach and his ability to teach autonomy and self-correction.

With your due diligence up to this point, now is the time to interview your child's prospective coach. Make an appointment to talk to the coach. Immediately before or between lessons is the worst time for a coach to be interviewed. Ask the prospective coach to describe his/her teaching philosophy. Evaluate the answers while considering how they may or may not match your child's developmental needs. Ask about updates on your child's progress, and the best way and time to contact the coach. Is it by e-mail, text message, or telephone? Ask if he/she has a recent background check mandated by many states and conducted by the state's Justice Department. You may be reluctant to ask this question, but a coach who has been involved with children will appreciate that you did.

Ask a coach about his/her playing and teaching background. At this developmental stage in your child's life, a coach's teaching competence is more important than his/her playing abilities. I personally know that many of the past top fifty tennis players in the world cannot coach, and I admit that fact. Ask if they have children or sisters or brothers. I always like to ask the coach a question concerning correcting behavior in his/her class. I also suggest asking how he/she would motivate an unmotivated child and if written goals are set for or by his/her students. Hopefully, after all these inquiries, you will have a good first impression of this coach.

After you have decided who will coach your child, it's important to support your child by attending practices when possible. Your child's progress, attentiveness, and effort can be observed. Children in this age group expect to have their parents' approval and praise after an activity. Before you give your child any feedback, first ask her if she had fun, and then ask how she feels she played. If you agree with her evaluation, then give her your approval. Do not praise your child if it is not warranted. Lessons should be accompanied by play dates for your child with other children in the group or a child preferably taught by the same coach to ensure the children are receiving the same information.

A Coach for the Next Skill Level

Selecting a coach, especially for intermediate- to advanced-level children who are eight to fifteen years old, is as important as selecting the best doctor to perform heart surgery on your child. Well, perhaps that is a bit of an exaggeration, but why wouldn't you want the best role model and teacher for your child's development? There is more at stake than enrolling in an activity just for the social experience. If your child has a negative experience with the wrong coach, she may be discouraged from participating in sports in general. A good coach, on the other hand, is like having another adult to help parent your child and teach skill sets that will be applied to multiple settings in life.

If your child has better-than-average grades, she may be a candidate for a partial or full college scholarship. Even if it doesn't lead to a professional career, it could open up other athletic job opportunities such as coaching or being a sports agent.

A child in a high-work-ethic and goal-setting sports environment can set the stage for future employment. I know, because years ago I was chosen by a nationally known children's charity as a director of fund-raising. I was told that my skills as a successful athlete and coach gave me an advantage over other similarly qualified professional fund-raisers. The comments I received indicated I was the successful candidate because:

- They knew that I could take the pressure of rejection;

- They felt that I had the work ethic needed to make good things happen; and

- They knew I had exhibited my ability to be both a team player and coach in sports that transfers into the workplace.

The way to select a coach at this level is to start the same way you did in the previous selection process. Don't ask only parents about coaches; also ask other coaches for their suggestions. For this ability level coaches should conduct practice lessons at the same pace at which matches are played. There is a saying that if you do not do it in practice, you will not be able to do it in competition. A creative and often-used approach at this level is to ask the prospective coach to evaluate your child's skill level and give you a detailed teaching implementation plan for you to consider.

What the evaluation should look like is a number of drills and sport-specific activities with the coach himself. The competition part of the evaluation is important because it's the only way to evaluate a player's mental approach to the game. This evaluation is an invaluable tool because it will give you a baseline of what factors to compare to the other coaches that you engage in this process. If the coach doesn't mention it, ask her about your child's mechanics. Proper mechanics in any sport are the first keys for a child to reach his/her maximum athletic potential.

An often-ignored aspect of development is a player's competitive behavior. By this, I mean how a child's behavior relates to his ability to cope with all aspects of being a competitive athlete. Ask the prospective coach to describe this area of your child's development. There will be a fee charged for the evaluation session and it is well worth the expenditure.

Other things to look for in a coach are:

- Motivates players and has fun teaching

- Low ratio of teacher to students

- Teaches mental strength

- Teaches sport awareness and how to manage games

- Assigns specific conditioning drills for your child

- Promotes playing sport with friends

- Conducts practices that replicate games

- Teaches players how to be self-reliant

- Takes an interest in developing each child's character

Besides the evaluation workout session, look for the coach to ask you about your child's grades, discipline, motivation, and work ethic. A coach may ask if you expect him to be at all your child's matches. Oftentimes, a coach has an assistant to watch his students' matches. This could be beneficial since the assistant's rate is usually less. Additionally, a coach trusts this person to observe all the details of the match, including parent involvement. If a coach asks if the child is currently being coached and why you are considering changing coaches, this is a good sign.

If you child has been diagnosed as having ADHD, you may want to ask a few more questions. Even if he has not been diagnosed but has challenges with learning, anxiety, depression, severe mood swings, motor, or phonic tics, more questions are suggested. Ask first if the coach is familiar with your child's specific condition. Then ask his/her philosophy in handling the situation if it becomes a distraction to the class.

After you engage the new coach, do not attempt to teach your child the sport without the coach's permission. It will inevitably frustrate both your child and the coach. I have watched many children quit a sport because of a parent's overzealous nature. I have also seen top coaches drop a child because of a parent's actions or reactions.

In elite coaching circles, do not be surprised if the coach asks you for your permission to visit another top coach for a second opinion concerning a specific aspect of your child's game. Often, the coach whose player has an issue that is concerning him might invite a coach whose opinion he respects to drop by a practice and observe the player. Or he may ask a coach to watch his player at a match or game.

Parent's Changing Role

At this juncture, your role as a parent is to be supportive of your child's efforts, as long as he has good focus and effort. In coaching circles, there is something that we call the "coaching triangle." The triangle has three components: the parent, the child, and the coach. In the beginning stages of sports, the control and responsibility weigh heavily with the parent. After all, parents choose the program, pay for the coaching and equipment, and are in charge of logistics for practices and games. The child in this stage basically is chauffeured, dressed (including having his shoestrings tied), and escorted to the playing area. The coach is in charge of teaching, discipline, and developing basic coordination, balance, and spatial skills for that sport. If the coach is a practicing dual-goal coach, life lessons will be taught.

When a young child reaches the advanced stage, parent responsibilities are mostly the same, except for tying the shoestrings. The child is now more responsible in all areas: equipment, clothing, packing water bottles, self-motivation, and improving in his/her skill sets during practices. The coach is more engaged because he is now invested in the child's progress, often for two reasons: he really cares for the child, and that child as a player is a reflection of the success of his program.

Normally, parents don't pick their child's high school or college coach. These coaches are in place. For the general student body in high school and college, academics and tuition are the determining factors in selection. However, a parent of a gifted athlete will strongly consider all options before the decision of where to send their child is made. Especially in individual sports, the coach and program are often the decisive factors.

Parents with children in college and the professional ranks morph into cheerleaders and extremely proud parents. My parents were no exception. In college and the professional ranks, coaches serve as emotional pillars to support their players' improvement in that sport. The onetime child is now entirely responsible for his own motivation, work ethic, and competitive ability, and hopefully will become a great role model for children.

CHAPTER ELEVEN
Final thoughts on Parenting – Game On!

The most important message I want to convey in this book is that parenting your child is 100 percent your responsibility, and the time you invest in the early years will help you build a deep, lasting connection with your child. Remember, there are other positive role models available to assist you. Parenting should not be left to chance or take a back seat to your job or other distractions. Be involved in your child's life. This takes time and hard work, and often means rearranging your priorities and sacrificing your own agenda. Be financially responsible, but more importantly, always be there for your child emotionally and physically.

With a parenting plan that both parents create and implement together, your dreams of being great parents can be realized. Seize the parenting opportunities that are presented to you. Oftentimes, you will have to create and seek new opportunities to reach the outcomes you wish for your child.

Central to the science of parenting is the environment created by the family in the home. When children are split between parents in two separate homes, the value of a good home environment doubles. Positive extended family members, teachers, family activities, and dual-goal coaches can have a significant role in your child's future as well. When parenting my own children, I wish I would have known what I have learned over the past fifty-plus years. Hindsight is so 20/20! However, it is never too late to develop a good relationship with them or your grandchildren and other family members.

My hope for you is that something in this book will resonate and help reach or reset your parenting goals. I hope it channels your interest or curiosity to be the best parent you can be. I hope it helps you explore a variety of activities that will aid in your child's development. Or perhaps it will confirm that your current style of parenting is working well for you and your child. As a child's primary role models, both parents share a very important role. Parenting does not have to be a lonely journey. It can be an exciting one, but only if you prepare yourself for unexpected situations that will arise.

Thoughts for parents:

- Stay in love with and be respectful of your spouse.

- Trust your spouse as your best friend.

- Stay true to yourself and true to your spouse.

- Spend quality time together

- Exercise together often.

- Cook together.

- Be caring and responsive to each other.

- Have healthy alcohol habits.

- Avoid smoking.

- Do not assume what your spouse is thinking; instead, ask him/her.

- Drive safely and defensively.

- Practice healthy conflict resolution.

- Grow with each other into a family.

- Be emotionally supportive of each other.

- Enjoy your work as a financial tool, but do not allow it to define your life.

- Be the best spouse on a day-to-day basis that you can be.

- Jointly with your spouse, write a detailed parenting plan for your child, which should include:

  - Family financial plan based on current income

  - Practice healthy nutrition for the entire family

  - Education for child

    - Start when child is three months old (chapter 6)

    - Both parents be a dual-goal parent

      - Develop cognitive skills

- Develop athletic skills

- Develop secure emotional environment

  ○ Teach manners

  ○ Take every opportunity to teach life lessons to your child

  ○ Schedule relief time from parenting

  ○ Include vacation and weekly family fun time

  ○ Monitor the progress and effectiveness of your parenting plan

- Change a parenting direction that is not working.

- Cherish family meals as a great setting to bond and share.

- Try to be relaxed; if you are anxious, your child may become anxious.

- Develop strong family relationships with all relatives that are available for your child, especially your child's grandparents, aunts, and uncles.

Thoughts about setting your family environment:

- We have noted the need for a secure and safe setting for your child's development; however, the same is needed for a strong marriage.

- Enjoy the gift of having a child and shaping his/her future potentials.

- Structure is great for family meals, study time, and bedtime for your child.

- Avoid having TV in a child's bedroom.

- Do not allow too much computer and electronic game time, if any, especially for children under six years old.

- Children should pick up their toys after playing with them.

- By example, keep the rest of the house in order.

- Have behavior guidelines and consequences for noncompliance.

- Let your child hear respectful conversations when you disagree with your spouse.

- Encourage your child to be inquisitive.

- Teach your child to be self-reliant at an early age.

- Let your child know that it's OK to make mistakes; even parents make mistakes.

- Apologize to your child when you make a mistake; it's good manners.

- Encourage your child to do the best he can in school and teach him proper study habits.

- Have fun playing games and doing activities with your child.

- Allow your child supervised play with a diversity of other children.

Thoughts about athletics and your child:

- Athletic skill sets will improve the quality of a child's life.

- Athletics will help a child's social development.

- Be your child's dual-goal coach, at least by the time she is three years old (chapter 6).

- It is never too late to start the games and activities in this book with your child to improve his athleticism.

- Sports are the best platform to learn how to cope with failure and develop good character traits.

- Take the opportunity to develop athletic skills with your child, but also yourself.

- Take advantage of the benefits to a child's brain development through athletics, sports, chess, music, play, and the arts.

- A child should play sports for his own sake, not the parents' sake.

- Effort and focus in any endeavor will foster improvement.

- Whether you win or not, sports are just a fun, healthy activity.

While few human challenges are greater than that of being a good parent, few experiences offer greater potential for fulfillment. The most rewarding of all human experiences is creating a good relationship with your child and spouse. There is no greater gift to your child than your sacrifice of intelligent parenting. Later in life, it becomes deeply gratifying to be able to reflect back on your effective responses to the challenges of parenthood.

I congratulate any parents who have overcome the unhelpful beliefs, misconceptions, and negative experiences of the way they were parented so that they can parent effectively. If you can do this, you have taken control of the most important job you'll ever have. Enjoy the journey, and cheers from one happy father, grandfather, and coach!

.

APPENDIX
A Guide to Begin Playing Chess with Your Child

———

Chess dates back fifteen hundred years and can be simply explained to children as a war game between two ancient armies. Engage kids by telling them that there are many paths to victory on the medieval chessboard battlefield. Although chess is often taught in a slow and intimidating manner, you can make learning a fun adventure. Break down the learning process by teaching your child the rules of movement for just one individual chess piece. Then introduce the other pieces and their movements—one at a time. This sequential approach will help a child memorize the possible moves for all the pieces so that the game can be played with greater confidence. Confidence is an important building block in childhood development and will stay with him into adulthood.

An important part of learning chess is applying reason and logic to the individual pieces' movements in order to organize attacks, structure defenses, and launch counterattacks. Being able to absorb information, and then correctly and quickly apply reason to solve problems, is as valuable in chess as it is in real-life situations. Learning chess should be fun, easy to understand, and conducted at a pace comfortable for each player. When chess knowledge is learned and practiced, the brain—like a muscle—can react more quickly and with greater accuracy.

Before starting to teach your child to play chess, it's important that you're comfortable with the movements of all the pieces and understand the basics of the game. This allows you to teach in a manner that is fun and rewarding. It's helpful to practice in advance before teaching your child. You only get one chance to make a first impression and you want your child's first exposure to the game to be fun. Be prepared to answer questions from your child that go beyond what you plan to teach at each session. And remember, it's OK for both you and your child to make mistakes.

The goal of chess is to capture the other army's king, usually by gaining advantage through capturing a greater number of high-value pieces. A capture occurs when an army piece lands on the space occupied by a piece of the opposing army. The captured piece is eliminated from the board. Always try to capture pieces of equal or greater value to gain an advantage over the opposing army.

Each army has six different categories of pieces, shown below in descending rank, with numbers in parentheses showing their point value. They are; king (infinite), queen (9), rooks (5), bishops (3), knights, (3), and pawns (1). These assigned numbers indicate their strength relative to one another.

Familiarize Yourself with the Chessboard
The chessboard battlefield is comprised of eight rows, eight squares deep. The rows' squares are alternately colored white and black in the same pattern as checkerboards.

The rows of squares running horizontally are called ranks, and those going vertically from top to bottom are called files. Rows of squares of the same color running in the same diagonal direction are called diagonals. The chessboard is placed between the two players so that, for each player, the rightmost square on the back rank is white.

Armies Set for Battle

A vinyl chessboard with two-inch squares works best for young players. The boards are portable, easy to clean, require less storage space than a wooden board, and are inexpensive. Most chessboards will have the ranks and files indicated on them, which will become helpful as children progress.

The chess pieces that you buy should be two inches in height for the pawns and taller for the other army pieces. Traditionally, chess pieces are black for one army and white for the opposing side. Children are attracted to colors. So in choosing each army's color, ask your child what two colors she would like for her special chess set (check online to see what colors are available so you will not disappoint your child if a certain color is not in stock). Having a child select her armies' colors will give her more buy-in to play her game. The large pieces are easier for small children to handle and assist in developing fine motor skills in the fingers.

Learning the Movement of Pieces with "Quarter-Board Games"
"Quarter-board games" refer to practice games played on any area of the chessboard that is one-quarter the size of the full board. Typically, you will use one corner of a chessboard, comprising an area four squares long by four squares deep. Starting small helps young players to more quickly understand and memorize the chess piece movements.

Quarter-board games should be played at last three to four times to provide a child experience in how the different pieces move and to help him retain what he's learning.

First, learn the movement options of the eight pawns:
The pawns are the foot soldiers on the chess battlefield. Pawns can only move straight forward; they can never move backward. On their very first move, pawns can move ahead either one or two spaces. On all subsequent moves, pawns can move only one square. Pawns can capture the opposing army's pieces only by moving diagonally one space. A pawn may not proceed straight ahead if it is blocked by another piece. It must either move diagonally and capture another piece or wait until the space ahead is cleared.

Moves for the Pawns

If a pawn reaches the opposite side of the board—the other army's first rank—it is promoted, and exchanged for any captured piece, usually the queen. Promoting is sometimes referred to as queening since exchanging for the most powerful piece on the board is overwhelmingly the choice made. Once a pawn lands on the opposing army's first rank, it is immediately promoted. On the next move, the opposing player's turn, the promoted piece can be captured. It is possible, though rare, to acquire multiple queens in your army through promotion. You could also promote a pawn to a piece such as a knight if the exchange were to result in a substantially improved position or a checkmate.

To solidify the pawn movements with your child, play a quarter-board game using just pawns. The focus of the quarter-board game with the pawns is to reinforce the beginning rule of one- or two-space movements as well as the diagonal capture.

Before you start the game with the pawn, ask your child to demonstrate to you the rules of movement, to gauge his/her level of understanding. Place four light-colored pawns in the back row of the four-square-by-four-square quarter-board and four dark-colored pawns on the opposite side. There should be two empty rows of squares between the armies.

The light-colored army always moves first. Have your child move the pawn to start your first quarter-board chess game. Congratulate your child on his understanding of the moves. Until he masters how all the pieces move, tell him often that it is OK to make mistakes. Be patient with your child by not telling him where to move. Rather, question moves that do not follow the rules of movement for that specific piece. This method speeds up the learning process of chess and does not make the child feel bad about making mistakes.

This process should be repeated with the introduction of each new piece until your child exhibits a comfort level in all the moves. Alternate with your child being the light-colored and then the dark-colored army.

Allow your child to experience moving first with the light army, as well as being the dark army and moving second.

Now introduce the rook, also known as the castle, to your child's army in the same way you introduced the pawn.

Second, learn the movement options of the two rooks:
The rooks move only straight on the ranks and files. They can move up to as many spaces that are empty or move through as many spaces to capture the other army's piece. They are actually the second most powerful pieces in the army, but are also the hardest to get into battle.

Moves for the Rooks

Play a quarter-board game with just the two armies' rooks. Set up the same way, placing the four castles in the four corners of your quarter-board. After your child achieves some competence with the movements of the rooks, prepare for his first full-board game with partial armies. Add all eight pawns in each army to the second rank of his army. Place the rooks in the back rank and on the square farthest to the right and to the left of the back rank. Now chess starts to get a little more complex and a lot more fun. Use the same positive verbal cues with the rooks that you used in teaching the movement of the pawns. First use the patient, slow pace. Gradually speed up the games to a faster pace. You can almost feel your child's brain expanding as you add army pieces! As a child's confidence increases, I find that he becomes more fascinated and enthralled with the game.

If your child is advanced in verbal skills and chess understanding, you can begin introducing the following questions to enhance her learning. Questions to ask before she moves:

1) What is your best move or best capture?

2) In moving pieces, are you leaving any other pieces open to capture?

3) Are any of your pieces about to be captured?

4) If yes, what is your best move to defend your army?

If for any reason any of these questions confuse your child or seem to slow down the learning process, wait until she can play with the full board to tackle these concepts. After learning how to move all her army's pieces, your child will be able to better answer these questions.

Third, learn the movement options of the two knights:
The knights are unique pieces and are the only ones in the army that can jump over other army pieces. They move in an L shape or a reverse L shape. The knight can move two squares in a straight line, then go either one square to the left or one square to the right. Or they can move one square in a straight line, then two squares either to the left or right. They do not move diagonally or straight along ranks and files. Knight moves also end on a square that is of the color opposite to the color of the square they started on.

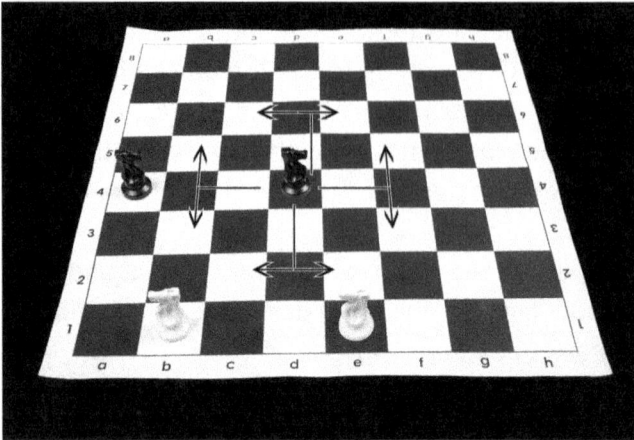

Moves for the Knights

Half-board games should be played first with just the two knights from each army, since there is not sufficient room in the quarter-board game to practice. After your child thoroughly understands the unique movement possibilities of the knights, play full-board games by adding the knights in their positions next to the rooks, along with the eight pawns. The goal of this phase of learning is to understand the rules of each army piece's movement. Note that moving forward, the pace of decision making becomes more important.

An important aspect of learning to play chess (and almost every subject) is to review previous lessons taught. Review will refresh a child's memory and motor skills. The essential ingredient to acquiring both mental and physical skills is repetition. Practicing a task repeatedly incorrectly will establish that incorrect task thinking and incorrect physical movement as being correct. Conversely, correct practice leads to correct performance.

Fourth, learn the movement options of the two bishops:
The bishops move diagonally along their original colored squares. White can only move on the white diagonal; black can only move along the black diagonal. Again, play half-board games, but now practice moving

just the two bishops from each army against each other. After your child practices the movement patterns for the bishops, add them to the back ranks next to the knights, along with the eight pawns in their positions along the second rank. At this point, play several movement games using the full board.

Moves for the Bishops

Fifth, learn the movement options of the queen:
The queen is the most powerful piece in your army. She is the most versatile member of the army, and as such, is the most sought-after piece to capture besides the king (which, once in checkmate, ends the game). The queen can move in any one continuous direction, either horizontally or vertically along the ranks and files (like rooks), or diagonally along whatever color she happens to be on (like bishops).

To ensure the understanding of the queen's rules of movement, play a quarter-board game with just the two queens. After your child shows competence and his pace has increased, he is ready to play on the full board. Add the queen to the full board with all the army's pieces, excluding the king. Play at least four quick (two-minute) practice games to ensure your child's understanding of movement patterns. Encourage quick movements of the pieces to keep the game fun and moving at a comfortable pace. Again, the goal of this phase of learning is to understand the rules of piece movement, not to win the game. Giving your child too much time to make a move may make him overthink the process. Keep the game moving at an even but flexible pace.

Moves for the Queen

During these two-minute practice games, move your army's pieces so your child can easily capture them. In short, make it easy for your child to be successful, but only at first. You will see a big smile on her face every time she captures your army's pieces. It is important for a child to succeed and feel confident in playing her first full board game, movement-wise, without the king on the board. A child will want to play more of the game if she experiences success. If your child continually gets beaten when she first tries the game, she will quit. Most children or adults will quit a new activity if it is either not fun or is embarrassing. As a child improves her game, increase the difficulty level so she remains challenged and feeling emotionally solid.

Sixth, learn the movement options of the king:
The king is the head of your army and deploys his forces in battle. The king can move only one square at a time, but in any direction. The king

must avoid capture by being placed in checkmate, which ends the game. Checkmate occurs when the king cannot move without being captured. The king cannot move into check.

Moves for the King

The last quarter-board games are played with the two kings. After a child displays competency, increase the pace of the quarter-board game. Add the king to his army and start to play with the full armies. As children and adults sometimes say before any competition, "Game on!"

Game On!
The light-colored army always moves first. The dark army then either moves to defend or attacks. Both sides usually move a few pawns as interference weapons first to create a wall effect to protect their king.

The first moves should also help your army control the center of the chessboard. Deploying the middle pawns in front of the queen and king helps achieve the initial tactical goal of controlling the center. Next, deploy the medium weapons: the knights and bishops. Then deploy the stronger weapons: the queen and rooks/castles. The object is not only to capture the other army's pieces, but also to gain a stronger battlefield position to trap the opponent's king in checkmate.

Castling

An advanced beginner move is castling. It is the only time when two pieces in the same army can move at the same time. Castling is a strong defensive move made to fortify the king's position and help keep him safe. If the king is not in check, it can be a handy escape move, too. I suggest that you introduce castling to the beginner after he develops competence in all the pieces' movement patterns.

The following rules apply to castling: Neither the king nor rook shall have moved before castling. No pieces may be between the king and rook, nor shall the king be in check. The king can perform the move with either rook.

To castle kingside, move the king to the right two spaces toward the rook. Then move the rook left two spaces to be on the other side of the king. To castle queenside, move the king two spaces to the left and the rook three spaces to the right. For castling, there is either a two- or three-space move. The movement of both pieces occurs as one move.

Ranks and Files

Allow me now to provide a little more information about the rank and file squares. Rank squares are identified on chessboards by letters, starting on the white army's left with the letter A. Moving from left to right, the second square to the right is B, and the lettering continues alphabetically until the eighth square, which is H. The black army on the opposite side of the board has its letters reversed to read H (on black's left) through A.

Files are identified with the numbers one through eight. The numbering starts with the white army's first (rank) square on the left side of the board. White's first square in the left corner is numbered one and continues to number eight, black's right-hand corner. The black army's far right side, rank square A, is designated files square eight.

Good luck with implementing chess as a wonderful developmental tool for your child and creating an activity that will be indelibly implanted in your minds forever!

www.ingramcontent.com/pod-product-compliance
Lightning Source LLC
LaVergne TN
LVHW021448080426
835509LV00018B/2201